Hands-On Python and

A Practical Guide to Deep Learning

Sarful Hassan

Preface

Welcome to *Hands-On Python and PyTorch: A Practical Guide to Deep Learning*. This book is designed to provide a comprehensive, hands-on learning experience in deep learning using Python and PyTorch. Whether you are a beginner looking to get started or an experienced developer aiming to enhance your skills, this book serves as a practical guide to mastering PyTorch for real-world AI applications.

Who This Book Is For

This book is intended for students, developers, researchers, and AI enthusiasts who want to gain a deeper understanding of deep learning using Python and PyTorch. Prior programming experience in Python is recommended, but not mandatory. If you are eager to explore neural networks, machine learning techniques, and AI model deployment, this book is for you.

How This Book Is Organized

The book is structured into multiple chapters, gradually increasing in complexity:

- **Chapters 1-7** introduce Python, PyTorch setup, and essential tensor operations.

- **Chapters 8-17** explore PyTorch's core functionalities, including neural networks, optimization techniques, and training configurations.

- **Chapters 18-26** cover advanced topics such as model parallelism, quantization, and distributed training.

- **Chapters 27-41** focus on practical applications in **computer vision, natural language processing (NLP), reinforcement learning, and real-world AI projects**.

Each chapter contains code examples and exercises to reinforce learning.

What Was Left Out

To keep the book practical and focused, some topics like detailed mathematical derivations and lower-level implementations of deep learning frameworks have been omitted. Instead, the book prioritizes hands-on implementation and practical applications.

Code Style (About the Code)

The code in this book follows best practices for Python and PyTorch development:

- Uses **Python 3.x** syntax.
- Code is formatted for **readability and efficiency**.
- Comments and explanations are included to clarify key concepts.
- Uses commonly accepted PyTorch conventions and best practices.

All code examples are tested and compatible with the latest PyTorch release at the time of writing.

Release Notes

This first edition provides a structured and practical introduction to PyTorch, covering a range of applications from basic deep learning to real-world AI model deployment.

Notes on the First Edition

This book represents a significant effort to compile practical knowledge and real-world applications for PyTorch learners. Feedback is welcome for future improvements and updates.

MechatronicsLAB Online Learning

For additional learning resources and support, visit our website:

- **Website:** mechatronicslab.net
- **Email:** mechatronicslab@gmail.com

Acknowledgments for the First Edition

Special thanks to everyone who contributed to the development of this book, including reviewers, technical editors, and the PyTorch community for their invaluable insights.

Copyright (MechatronicsLAB)

Disclaimer

The information in this book is provided for educational and informational purposes only. While every effort has been made to ensure accuracy, the author and publisher make no warranties regarding the completeness, reliability, or applicability of the content. The reader is responsible for ensuring proper implementation and adherence to licensing regulations for PyTorch and other related tools.

Table of Contents

Chapter - 1 Introduction to Python and PyTorch

Python and PyTorch are a powerful combination for deep learning and machine learning applications. Together, they provide a flexible and efficient framework for building, training, and deploying neural networks and other machine learning models.

Why Python?

Python has become the de facto language for machine learning and data science due to its:

1. **Ease of Learning**: Python's simple and intuitive syntax allows beginners to focus on learning concepts rather than grappling with complex code.
2. **Rich Ecosystem**: Python's libraries, such as NumPy, Pandas, and Matplotlib, integrate seamlessly with PyTorch to streamline data manipulation and visualization.
3. **Extensive Community Support**: Python boasts a vast and active community, ensuring that resources, tutorials, and libraries are always available.

What is PyTorch?

PyTorch is an open-source deep learning framework developed by Facebook's AI Research lab (FAIR). It has gained immense popularity due to its dynamic computation graph, ease of use, and extensive capabilities for research and production.

Key Features of PyTorch

1. **Dynamic Computation Graphs**:
    a. Unlike static graph frameworks, PyTorch builds computation graphs dynamically during runtime, offering greater flexibility and ease of debugging.
2. **Ease of Use**:
    a. PyTorch's intuitive API and Pythonic design make it user-friendly and accessible to both beginners and experts.
3. **Autograd Module**:
    a. The automatic differentiation engine computes gradients efficiently, simplifying backpropagation and optimization

tasks.

4. **Rich Ecosystem**:
    a. Includes libraries like TorchVision (for computer vision), TorchText (for NLP), and TorchAudio (for audio processing).
5. **GPU Acceleration**:
    a. Built-in support for CUDA accelerates computations on GPUs, making it suitable for large-scale deep learning tasks.
6. **Scalability**:
    a. PyTorch supports both research and production workflows, with features like TorchScript and PyTorch Lightning for scaling projects.

Why Use Python with PyTorch?

1. **Native Integration**: PyTorch is built with Python in mind, making it seamless to use with Python's scientific computing libraries.
2. **Rapid Prototyping**: The dynamic nature of PyTorch, combined with Python's simplicity, allows for fast experimentation and debugging.
3. **Community and Support**: PyTorch's active community and extensive documentation provide unparalleled support for Python developers.

Applications of Python and PyTorch

1. **Computer Vision**:
    a. Image classification, object detection, and semantic segmentation.
2. **Natural Language Processing (NLP)**:
    a. Sentiment analysis, machine translation, and text generation.
3. **Reinforcement Learning**:
    a. Training agents for decision-making tasks in gaming and robotics.
4. **Time-Series Forecasting**:
    a. Predicting trends and patterns in sequential data, such as stock prices or weather.
5. **Generative Models**:

a. Creating GANs (Generative Adversarial Networks) for generating realistic images, videos, and more.
6. **Healthcare**:
   a. Building models for diagnostic imaging, drug discovery, and patient outcome prediction.
7. **Autonomous Systems**:
   a. Training models for self-driving cars and drones.

Python and PyTorch offer a robust foundation for exploring and implementing machine learning solutions. Whether you're a researcher, developer, or enthusiast, this combination empowers you to tackle complex challenges with efficiency and creativity.

Chapter-2 Installing and Setting Up PyTorch

Setting up PyTorch is straightforward, with support for various platforms, including Windows, Linux, and macOS. This guide provides detailed steps to ensure a smooth installation process tailored to your system.

Step 1: Verify Python Installation Ensure Python is installed on your system. Follow these steps:
1. Check if Python is installed: `python --version`
   If Python is not installed, download it from the official Python website and install it. During installation, ensure the option to add Python to your system PATH is selected.
2. Verify pip (Python's package manager) is installed: `pip --version`
   If pip is missing, install it: `python -m ensurepip --upgrade`

Step 2: Determine Your Configuration PyTorch provides different installation commands based on your:
- **Operating System**: Windows, Linux, or macOS.
- **Package Manager**: Pip or Conda.
- **CUDA Version**: Determines GPU acceleration support.

Visit the PyTorch Installation Page and use the interactive selector to find the exact command for your configuration.

Step 3: Install PyTorch Select the installation method that matches your system:

Using Pip:

- For CPU-only support: `pip install torch torchvision torchaudio`
- For GPU support (e.g., CUDA 11.8): `pip install torch torchvision torchaudio --index-url`

Using Conda:

- For CPU-only support: `conda install pytorch torchvision torchaudio cpuonly -c pytorch`
- For GPU support: `conda install pytorch torchvision torchaudio pytorch-cuda=11.8 -c pytorch -c nvidia`

Installing from Source: For advanced users who need the latest features or custom builds:

1. Clone the PyTorch repository: `git clone --recursive` https://github.com/pytorch/pytorch

2. Build and install PyTorch: `cd pytorch python setup.py install`

Step 4: Verify Installation After installation, verify PyTorch by running the following commands in a Python interpreter:

```
import torch
print("PyTorch version:", torch.__version__)
print("CUDA available:",
torch.cuda.is_available())
```

Output should display the PyTorch version and whether CUDA support is available.**nstalling PyTorch on Different Platforms**

Windows:

- Ensure Python and pip are updated.
- Use pip to install PyTorch. For GPU acceleration, ensure your GPU drivers and CUDA Toolkit are installed and compatible.

Linux:

- Use the pip or conda commands for installation.
- For GPU users, verify that NVIDIA drivers and the correct CUDA Toolkit are installed. `nvidia-smi nvcc --version`

- Consider using Docker for isolated environments.

macOS:
- PyTorch supports macOS natively. Install using pip or conda.
- GPU support is limited to Metal Performance Shaders (MPS) for Macs with Apple Silicon.

Anaconda:
1. Create a new environment: `conda create -n pytorch_env python=3.9`
   `conda activate pytorch_env`
2. Install PyTorch using conda commands listed above.

Step 5: Install Supporting Libraries For a better development experience, install additional libraries:
- **NumPy**: Essential for numerical operations. `pip install numpy`
- **Matplotlib**: For data visualization. `pip install matplotlib`
- **Jupyter Notebook**: For interactive development. `pip install notebook`

Step 6: Test PyTorch Run the following script to ensure PyTorch is functioning correctly:

```
import torch
def test_pytorch():
    x = torch.rand(5, 3)
    print("Random Tensor:", x)
    if torch.cuda.is_available():
        print("CUDA is available. Running on GPU.")
        device = torch.device("cuda")
        x = x.to(device)
    else:
        print("CUDA is not available. Running on CPU.")
    print("Tensor after transfer:", x)
test_pytorch()
```

Expected output includes the generated random tensor and whether CUDA support is available.

Common Troubleshooting Tips
1. **Missing Dependencies**: Ensure pip or conda is up to date:

```
pip install --upgrade pip
conda update conda
```

2. **CUDA Compatibility Issues**: Verify your GPU drivers and CUDA Toolkit version match PyTorch's requirements.
3. **Installation Errors**: Ensure your Python version is compatible (3.7 or higher)

With PyTorch installed and tested, you're ready to explore deep learning with one of the most flexible and powerful frameworks available!

Chapter-3 Overview of PyTorch's Design and Ecosystem

PyTorch is one of the leading frameworks for deep learning, offering unparalleled flexibility, usability, and performance. Its dynamic computation graph and robust ecosystem make it suitable for a wide range of applications, from academic research to industrial deployment.

Core Design Principles of PyTorch
1. **Dynamic Computation Graphs**:
   a. PyTorch builds computation graphs on-the-fly during runtime. This makes debugging and experimentation more intuitive compared to static graph frameworks.
   b. Flexible graph creation allows for dynamic input sizes and control structures, such as loops and conditionals.
2. **Ease of Use**:
   a. PyTorch's Pythonic interface ensures a smooth learning curve for developers and researchers.
   b. Intuitive APIs simplify tasks like tensor manipulation, model creation, and training loops.
3. **Native GPU Support**:
   a. Seamless integration with CUDA allows for efficient computation on NVIDIA GPUs.
   b. Users can easily move data and models between CPUs and GPUs.

4. **Modularity and Customization**:
    a. PyTorch allows users to modify and extend its components, such as datasets, layers, and training routines.
    b. Built-in support for creating custom layers and models.
5. **Strong Autograd Engine**:
    a. The autograd module automatically computes gradients for tensor operations, simplifying backpropagation.
    b. Supports complex architectures like recurrent neural networks (RNNs) and transformers.

PyTorch Ecosystem

The PyTorch ecosystem includes a variety of libraries and tools that extend its functionality:

1. **TorchVision**:
    a. Designed for computer vision tasks.
    b. Includes datasets like CIFAR-10, ImageNet, and COCO.
    c. Pre-trained models for classification, detection, and segmentation (e.g., ResNet, Faster R-CNN).
2. **TorchText**:
    a. Optimized for natural language processing (NLP).
    b. Tools for tokenization, embedding, and dataset preprocessing.
    c. Supports datasets like IMDB, WikiText, and others.
3. **TorchAudio**:
    a. Focused on audio and speech processing.
    b. Features tools for loading, transforming, and augmenting audio data.
    c. Pre-trained models for tasks like speech recognition and audio classification.
4. **PyTorch Lightning**:
    a. A higher-level library built on PyTorch.
    b. Simplifies training workflows while maintaining flexibility for customization.
    c. Supports multi-GPU and distributed training out of the box.

5. **TorchServe**:
    a. A framework for deploying PyTorch models in production.
    b. Features include multi-model serving, metrics, and logging.
6. **Hugging Face Transformers**:
    a. Provides pre-trained transformer models for NLP tasks.
    b. Seamless integration with PyTorch for fine-tuning and inference.
7. **Detectron2**:
    a. A library for object detection and segmentation.
    b. Built by Facebook AI, it extends PyTorch for advanced vision tasks.
8. **PyTorch Geometric**:
    a. Focused on graph neural networks (GNNs).
    b. Supports tasks like node classification and graph embedding.

Advantages of PyTorch's Ecosystem
1. **Interoperability**:
    a. Components of the PyTorch ecosystem integrate seamlessly with one another.
    b. Compatibility with external libraries such as NumPy, Pandas, and Matplotlib.
2. **State-of-the-Art Research**:
    a. PyTorch is the framework of choice for many academic papers and research projects.
    b. Frequent updates ensure cutting-edge features are available.
3. **Production Ready**:
    a. Tools like TorchServe and ONNX simplify deploying PyTorch models in production environments.
    b. PyTorch's robust API ensures reliability for industrial applications.
4. **Extensive Community Support**:
    a. A large and active community contributes to tutorials, repositories, and extensions.

      b.   Collaboration with industry leaders ensures rapid growth and innovation.

Applications of PyTorch
1. **Computer Vision**:
   a. Image classification, object detection, and style transfer.
2. **Natural Language Processing (NLP)**:
   a. Sentiment analysis, text generation, and machine translation.
3. **Reinforcement Learning**:
   a. Training agents for tasks in robotics, gaming, and simulation environments.
4. **Generative Models**:
   a. Building GANs (Generative Adversarial Networks) for creating images, videos, and audio.
5. **Healthcare**:
   a. Developing diagnostic models for medical imaging and patient data analysis.
6. **Graph Neural Networks (GNNs)**:
   a. Applications in recommendation systems, molecular property prediction, and social network analysis.

PyTorch's design and ecosystem make it a versatile tool for deep learning practitioners. Whether you are conducting cutting-edge research or deploying AI systems at scale, PyTorch provides the tools and flexibility to succeed.

Chapter-4 Key Concepts: Tensors, Autograd, and Modules in PyTorch

PyTorch is built around three fundamental concepts that form the backbone of its deep learning capabilities: Tensors, Autograd, and Modules. Understanding these concepts is crucial for effectively using PyTorch in your projects.

1. Tensors
Tensors are the fundamental data structure in PyTorch. They are multi-

dimensional arrays similar to NumPy arrays but with additional features for GPU acceleration.

Key Features of Tensors:

- **Multi-dimensional**: Support for scalars, vectors, matrices, and higher-order tensors.
- **GPU Acceleration**: Seamless computation on GPUs using CUDA.
- **Dynamic Typing**: Support for various data types like float, int, and bool.
- **Broadcasting**: Enables operations on tensors of different shapes, aligning them automatically.

Creating Tensors:

```
import torch

# Create tensors
x = torch.tensor([1.0, 2.0, 3.0])          # 1D tensor
y = torch.zeros(3, 3)                       # 2D tensor
with zeros
z = torch.rand(2, 4)                        # Random 2x4
tensor

# Perform operations
result = x + 2                              # Element-wise
addition
product = x * 3                             # Element-wise
multiplication
```

Moving Tensors to GPU:

```
device = torch.device("cuda" if
torch.cuda.is_available() else "cpu")
x = x.to(device)
```

2. Autograd

Autograd is PyTorch's automatic differentiation engine. It computes gradients for tensor operations, enabling efficient backpropagation in neural networks.

How Autograd Works:

- PyTorch records operations performed on tensors with requires_grad=True.

- The `.backward()` function computes gradients and stores them in the `.grad` attribute of tensors.
- Supports dynamic computation graphs for flexibility during runtime.

Example:

```
# Enable gradient computation
a = torch.tensor([2.0, 3.0], requires_grad=True)
b = a ** 2 + 3 * a
# Compute gradients
b.sum().backward()
print(a.grad)   # Output: Gradients of 'a'
```

Detaching Tensors: Detach tensors to prevent gradient computation:

```
x_no_grad = x.detach()
```

3. Modules

Modules in PyTorch represent layers or models. They are instances of the `torch.nn.Module` class and are used to define, organize, and train neural networks.

Defining a Custom Module:

```
import torch.nn as nn
class SimpleModel(nn.Module):
    def __init__(self):
        super(SimpleModel, self).__init__()
        self.layer1 = nn.Linear(10, 5)
        self.layer2 = nn.ReLU()
        self.layer3 = nn.Linear(5, 1)
    def forward(self, x):
        x = self.layer1(x)
        x = self.layer2(x)
        x = self.layer3(x)
        return x
# Instantiate and use the model
model = SimpleModel()
x = torch.rand(10)
output = model(x)
```

Predefined Modules: PyTorch provides a wide range of predefined modules in `torch.nn` for building neural networks:

- **Linear Layers**: nn.Linear
- **Activation Functions**: nn.ReLU, nn.Sigmoid
- **Convolutional Layers**: nn.Conv2d
- **Pooling Layers**: nn.MaxPool2d
- **Recurrent Layers**: nn.RNN, nn.LSTM, nn.GRU

Optimizing Models:

Use `torch.optim` to optimize the model:

```
import torch.optim as optim

optimizer = optim.SGD(model.parameters(), lr=0.01)

# Training loop example
loss_fn = nn.MSELoss()
for epoch in range(10):
    optimizer.zero_grad()  # Clear previous gradients
    predictions = model(x)
    loss = loss_fn(predictions, torch.tensor([1.0]))
    loss.backward()        # Compute gradients
    optimizer.step()       # Update parameters
```

Summary

- **Tensors**: PyTorch's core data structure for computation, offering GPU acceleration and dynamic operations.
- **Autograd**: Automatic differentiation for easy backpropagation.
- **Modules**: Building blocks for creating and training neural networks.

Understanding these concepts will help you effectively use PyTorch for developing and deploying machine learning models.

Chapter – 5 Tensor Operations and Broadcasting in PyTorch

PyTorch provides a comprehensive framework for tensor manipulation and broadcasting, essential for implementing machine learning models and deep learning pipelines. Understanding tensor operations and broadcasting rules simplifies handling multi-dimensional data, enabling efficient computations and model training. This chapter explores tensor operations, broadcasting, and best practices for their usage in PyTorch.

Key Characteristics of Tensor Operations in PyTorch:

- **Multi-dimensional Arrays:** Tensors generalize vectors and matrices to higher dimensions.
- **Rich Operations:** Supports arithmetic, indexing, slicing, and advanced matrix operations.
- **Broadcasting:** Aligns tensors with different shapes for element-wise operations.
- **GPU Acceleration:** Enables high-speed computations with CUDA tensors.

Basic Rules for Tensor Broadcasting:

1. **Alignment from Right:** Tensors align their shapes from the trailing dimension.
2. **Compatible Dimensions:** Dimensions are compatible if they are equal or one of them is 1.
3. **Resulting Shape:** The result has the maximum size in each dimension.
4. **Singleton Expansion:** Dimensions of size 1 are expanded to match the larger dimension

Syntax Table:

SL No	Function	Syntax/Example	Description
1	Tensor Creation	`torch.tensor(data)`	Creates a tensor from data.
2	Element-wise Operations	`tensor1 + tensor2`	Performs addition with broadcasting support.
3	Tensor Reshaping	`tensor.view(shape)`	Changes the shape of a tensor.
4	Advanced Indexing	`tensor[indices]`	Accesses specific elements of a tensor.
5	Matrix Multiplication	`torch.matmul(tensor1, tensor2)`	Performs matrix multiplication.

Syntax Explanation:

1. Tensor Creation

What is Tensor Creation?

Creating tensors is the first step in working with PyTorch. Tensors are multi-dimensional arrays used to store data and parameters in models.

Syntax:

```
import torch
tensor = torch.tensor([[1, 2], [3, 4]])
```

Detailed Explanation:

- **Purpose:** Initializes a tensor with specified data.
- **Parameters:**
  - `data`: Nested lists, tuples, or arrays representing the tensor's elements.
- **Output:** A PyTorch tensor with the specified values. Tensors can

represent various data types, and their behavior can be controlled by specifying dtype.

Example:

```
tensor = torch.tensor([[1, 2], [3, 4]])
print(tensor)
```

Example Explanation:

- Creates a 2x2 tensor with elements [1, 2, 3, 4].
- Outputs: tensor([[1, 2],
               [3, 4]])

2. Element-wise Operations

What are Element-wise Operations?

Element-wise operations apply arithmetic functions across all elements of two tensors, supporting broadcasting.

Syntax:

```
result = tensor1 + tensor2
```

Detailed Explanation:

- **Purpose:** Adds, subtracts, multiplies, or divides tensors element-wise.
- **Broadcasting:** Automatically aligns shapes of tensors to facilitate the operation.
- **Behavior:** If the tensors do not have the same shape, broadcasting rules are applied to align dimensions by expanding singleton dimensions (dimensions of size 1) to match the corresponding dimension of the other tensor.
- **Output:** A tensor resulting from applying the operation to aligned tensors.

Example:

```
tensor1 = torch.tensor([[1, 2], [3, 4]])
tensor2 = torch.tensor([[5], [6]])
result = tensor1 + tensor2
print(result)
```

Example Explanation:

- Adds a 2x2 tensor and a 2x1 tensor via broadcasting.
- Outputs: tensor([[6, 7],
               [9, 10]])

3. Tensor Reshaping

What is Tensor Reshaping?

Reshaping changes a tensor's shape without altering its data.

Syntax:

```
reshaped = tensor.view(new_shape)
```

Detailed Explanation:

- **Purpose:** Adjusts tensor dimensions to meet specific requirements, such as preparing data for a neural network.
- **Parameters:**
    - new_shape: A tuple specifying the desired shape of the tensor. The product of the new shape must match the total number of elements in the original tensor.
- **Behavior:** The view method provides a new view of the tensor, sharing the same underlying data without creating a copy.
- **Output:** A tensor with the specified shape. Incompatible shapes result in a runtime error.

Example:

```
tensor = torch.tensor([1, 2, 3, 4])
reshaped = tensor.view(2, 2)
print(reshaped)
```

Example Explanation:

- Converts a 1D tensor into a 2x2 tensor.
- Outputs: tensor([[1, 2],
            [3, 4]])

4. Advanced Indexing

What is Advanced Indexing?

Advanced indexing extracts specific elements or subarrays from a tensor.

Syntax:

```
element = tensor[indices]
```

Detailed Explanation:

- **Purpose:** Accesses elements or slices of tensors using index values, masks, or advanced patterns.
- **Indexing Options:**
    - Integer indexing: Accesses a single element.

        o   Slicing: Accesses a range of elements.

        o   Boolean indexing: Filters elements based on conditions.

- **Behavior:** Provides flexibility to select, modify, or analyze parts of a tensor efficiently.
- **Output:** A tensor or scalar value based on the specified indexing method.

Example:
```
tensor = torch.tensor([[1, 2], [3, 4]])
print(tensor[1, 0])
```
Example Explanation:
- Accesses the element at row 1, column 0 (value 3).
- Outputs: `tensor(3)`

5. Matrix Multiplication

What is Matrix Multiplication?
Matrix multiplication calculates the dot product between corresponding rows and columns of two tensors.
Syntax:
```
result = torch.matmul(tensor1, tensor2)
```
Detailed Explanation:
- **Purpose:** Computes the product of two tensors following the rules of matrix algebra.
- **Parameters:**
  - o   `tensor1`, `tensor2`: Input tensors where the inner dimensions must match for valid multiplication.
- **Behavior:** Supports 1D (vector), 2D (matrix), and higher-dimensional tensor multiplication using batch processing.
- **Output:** The resulting tensor has dimensions that combine the outer dimensions of the inputs.

Example:
```
tensor1 = torch.tensor([[1, 2], [3, 4]])
tensor2 = torch.tensor([[5, 6], [7, 8]])
result = torch.matmul(tensor1, tensor2)
print(result)
```
Example Explanation:

- Multiplies two 2x2 tensors.
- Outputs: `tensor([[19, 22],`
            `[43, 50]])`

Real-Life Project:

Project Name: Image Transformation with Tensor Broadcasting

Project Goal: Perform operations like scaling, rotation, and translation on image tensors using broadcasting.

Code for This Project:

```
import torch

# Create a sample image tensor (3x3 grayscale)
image = torch.tensor([[0.1, 0.2, 0.3],
                      [0.4, 0.5, 0.6],
                      [0.7, 0.8, 0.9]])

# Scaling operation
scale = torch.tensor([2.0])
scaled_image = image * scale

# Translation operation
translation = torch.tensor([[0.1], [0.2], [0.3]])
translated_image = image + translation

print("Scaled Image:")
print(scaled_image)
print("\nTranslated Image:")
print(translated_image)
```

Expected Output:

- **Scaled Image:**

```
tensor([[0.2, 0.4, 0.6],
        [0.8, 1.0, 1.2],
        [1.4, 1.6, 1.8]])
```

- **Translated Image:**

```
tensor([[0.2, 0.3, 0.4],
        [0.6, 0.7, 0.8],
        [1.0, 1.1, 1.2]])
```

Chapter - 6 Indexing, Slicing, and Reshaping Tensors in PyTorch

Indexing, slicing, and reshaping are fundamental operations in PyTorch, enabling efficient manipulation and transformation of tensors. These operations are crucial for preprocessing data, extracting subarrays, and structuring tensors to fit model requirements. This chapter provides an in-depth exploration of these tensor operations in PyTorch.

Key Characteristics of Tensor Operations in PyTorch:

- **Indexing:** Access specific elements, rows, or columns of tensors.
- **Slicing:** Extract subarrays using range specifications.
- **Reshaping:** Change the shape of a tensor without altering its data.
- **Advanced Operations:** Combine indexing, slicing, and reshaping for complex tensor manipulations.

Basic Tensor Manipulation Rules:

1. **0-based Indexing:** Tensors use zero-based indexing, similar to Python lists.
2. **Shape Consistency:** Ensure the reshaped tensor's total elements match the original.
3. **Negative Indexing:** Negative indices access elements from the end.
4. **Slicing Syntax:** Use `start:end:step` for slicing.
5. **Broadcasting Compatibility:** Reshape tensors to align dimensions for operations.

Syntax Table:

SL No	Function	Syntax/Example	Description
1	Access Elements	`tensor[index]`	Retrieves specific elements.
2	Slice Tensor	`tensor[start:end]`	Extracts a subarray of the tensor.
3	Reshape Tensor	`tensor.view(shape)` or `tensor.reshape(sh`	Changes the shape of a tensor.

		ape)	
4	Access Rows/Col umns	`tensor[row, col]`	Accesses rows or columns in multi-dimensional tensors.
5	Combine Operation s	`tensor[start:end] .view(shape)`	Combines slicing and reshaping.

Syntax Explanation:

1. Access Elements

What is Accessing Elements?
Accessing elements is the process of retrieving individual or specific groups of values from a tensor. This operation is fundamental for data analysis and manipulation, as it allows selective extraction of data points.
Syntax:
```
value = tensor[index]
```
Detailed Explanation:
- **Purpose:** Retrieves a single element or a subarray from a tensor for inspection, computation, or further manipulation.
- **Parameters:**
  - `index`: Specifies the position(s) of the element(s) to retrieve. It can be an integer, a tuple for multi-dimensional tensors, or a slice object.
- **Behavior:**
  - Positive indices count from the start of the tensor (0-based).
  - Negative indices count backward from the end of the tensor.
  - Indexing a single element returns a scalar tensor.
- **Output:** The accessed tensor element(s) as a scalar or a tensor.
Example:
```
import torch
tensor = torch.tensor([10, 20, 30, 40])
value = tensor[2]
print(value)
```

Example Explanation:
- Accesses the third element (index 2) of the tensor.
- Outputs: `tensor(30)`

2. Slice Tensor

What is Slicing a Tensor?
Slicing a tensor refers to extracting a contiguous portion of a tensor by specifying a range of indices. This is useful for tasks such as cropping data, dividing datasets, or focusing on specific regions of interest within a tensor.

Syntax:
```
slice = tensor[start:end]
```

Detailed Explanation:
- **Purpose:** Selects a sequence of elements from a tensor, defined by start and end indices, for targeted analysis or preprocessing.
- **Parameters:**
  - `start`: Index to begin the slice (inclusive). Defaults to 0 if not specified.
  - `end`: Index to stop the slice (exclusive). Defaults to the size of the tensor along the sliced dimension if not specified.
  - `step`: Interval between indices in the slice. Defaults to 1 if not specified.
- **Behavior:**
  - Generates a view of the original tensor (no new memory allocation).
  - Negative indices and steps allow flexible extraction, such as reverse slicing.
- **Output:** A subarray of the tensor as specified by the slicing parameters.

Example:
```
tensor = torch.tensor([1, 2, 3, 4, 5])
slice = tensor[1:4]
print(slice)
```

Example Explanation:
- Extracts elements from index 1 to 3.
- Outputs: `tensor([2, 3, 4])`

3. Reshape Tensor

What is Reshaping a Tensor?
Reshaping a tensor changes its structure while keeping the data intact. This operation is crucial for preparing data to meet the requirements of machine learning models or computational tasks.

Syntax:
```
reshaped = tensor.view(shape)
```

Detailed Explanation:
- **Purpose:** Adjusts the dimensions of a tensor to align with specific processing requirements.
- **Parameters:**
  - `shape`: A tuple representing the desired shape. The product of the shape dimensions must match the total number of elements in the tensor.
- **Behavior:**
  - `view`: Creates a new view of the tensor without copying data.
  - `reshape`: Performs the same task but can allocate new memory if necessary.
  - Use `-1` as a dimension in the shape to automatically infer its value.
- **Output:** A tensor with the specified shape, ready for downstream tasks.

Example:
```
tensor = torch.tensor([1, 2, 3, 4, 5, 6])
reshaped = tensor.view(2, 3)
print(reshaped)
```

Example Explanation:
- Converts a 1D tensor of size 6 into a 2x3 tensor.
- Outputs: `tensor([[1, 2, 3],`
           `[4, 5, 6]])`

4. Access Rows/Columns

What is Accessing Rows or Columns?
Accessing rows or columns involves isolating specific dimensions of a multi-dimensional tensor. This is vital for operations like feature extraction or filtering in machine learning tasks.

Syntax:
```
row = tensor[row_index]
column = tensor[:, col_index]
```

Detailed Explanation:
- **Purpose:** Extracts specific rows or columns to analyze particular features or dimensions in a dataset.
- **Parameters:**
  - row_index: Specifies the index of the row to extract.
  - col_index: Specifies the index of the column to extract across all rows.
- **Behavior:**
  - A single index returns a row or column as a lower-dimensional tensor.
  - Combines indexing and slicing to facilitate targeted extraction.
  - Supports negative indexing for reverse access.
- **Output:** A 1D tensor representing the selected row or column.

Example:
```
tensor = torch.tensor([[1, 2, 3], [4, 5, 6], [7, 8, 9]])
row = tensor[1]
column = tensor[:, 2]
print(row)
print(column)
```

Example Explanation:
- Extracts the second row and third column of the tensor.
- Outputs: tensor([4, 5, 6])
  tensor([3, 6, 9]

5. Combine Operations

What is Combining Operations?
Combining operations applies multiple tensor manipulations, such as slicing and reshaping, in a single pipeline. This approach simplifies complex preprocessing workflows.

Syntax:
```
result = tensor[start:end].view(new_shape)
```

Detailed Explanation:
- **Purpose:** Streamlines tensor transformations by chaining operations, reducing the need for intermediate variables.
- **Parameters:**
  - start, end: Indices for slicing to extract a specific portion of the tensor.
  - new_shape: Desired shape of the resulting tensor. Must be compatible with the total elements in the sliced tensor.
- **Behavior:** Executes slicing first, followed by reshaping, to produce the desired tensor structure.
- **Output:** The transformed tensor ready for further computation or analysis.

Example:
```
tensor = torch.tensor([1, 2, 3, 4, 5, 6])
result = tensor[1:5].view(2, 2)
print(result)
```

Example Explanation:
- Slices the tensor from index 1 to 4 and reshapes it into a 2x2 tensor.
- Outputs: tensor([[2, 3],
              [4, 5]])

Real-Life Project:
Project Name: Reshaping and Analyzing Image Data
Project Goal: Preprocess and analyze image tensors by slicing and reshaping for model input.

Code for This Project:

```
import torch
# Create a sample image tensor (4x4 grayscale)
image = torch.tensor([[1, 2, 3, 4],
                      [5, 6, 7, 8],
                      [9, 10, 11, 12],
                      [13, 14, 15, 16]])
# Slice and reshape
cropped = image[1:3, 1:3]
reshaped = cropped.view(1, 4)
print("Cropped Image:")
print(cropped)
print("\nReshaped Tensor:")
print(reshaped)
```

Expected Output:

- **Cropped Image:**

```
tensor([[ 6,  7],
        [10, 11]])
```

- **Reshaped Tensor:**

```
tensor([[ 6,  7, 10, 11]])
```

Chapter - 7 Performing Mathematical Operations with Tensors in PyTorch

Mathematical operations are fundamental in PyTorch, enabling efficient computation for machine learning and deep learning tasks. PyTorch provides a wide array of mathematical functions that operate on tensors, such as element-wise operations, reductions, matrix operations, and more. This chapter explores various mathematical operations and how they are implemented with tensors in PyTorch.

Key Characteristics of Mathematical Operations in PyTorch:
- **Element-wise Operations:** Perform arithmetic computations on individual tensor elements.
- **Reduction Operations:** Compute summary statistics such as sums, means, and maximum values.
- **Matrix Operations:** Enable linear algebra operations like dot products, matrix multiplication, and decompositions.
- **Broadcasting:** Allows operations on tensors of different shapes by automatically expanding dimensions.
- **In-place Operations:** Modify tensors directly to save memory and improve performance.

Basic Rules for Tensor Mathematics:
1. **Shape Compatibility:** Shapes must align or be broadcastable for operations.
2. **In-place Operations:** Use an underscore (e.g., add_) for operations that modify tensors in place.
3. **Type Casting:** Ensure tensors have compatible data types for operations.
4. **Precision:** Use float32 or float64 for higher precision in computations.

Syntax Table:

SL No	Function	Syntax/Example	Description
1	Element-wise Addition	`tensor1 + tensor2`	Adds two tensors element-wise.
2	Reduction Operation	`tensor.sum()`	Computes the sum of all elements.
3	Matrix Multiplication	`torch.matmul(tensor1, tensor2)`	Performs matrix multiplication.
4	Transpose	`tensor.T` or `tensor.transpose(dim0, dim1)`	Transposes a tensor along specified dimensions.
5	In-place Addition	`tensor.add_(value)`	Adds a value to tensor elements in place.

Syntax Explanation:

1. Element-wise Addition

What is Element-wise Addition?
Element-wise addition is the process of adding corresponding elements of two tensors. This operation is useful for computations like adjusting weights, adding biases, or combining results.
Syntax:
`result = tensor1 + tensor2`
Detailed Explanation:
- **Purpose:** Adds two tensors element-wise to produce a tensor of the same shape.
- **Parameters:**
    - tensor1, tensor2: Input tensors that must have the same shape or be broadcastable.
- **Behavior:**
    - If the shapes do not match, PyTorch applies broadcasting rules to align the shapes.

- The operation does not modify the input tensors unless performed in place.
- **Output:** A new tensor containing the element-wise sums.

Example:

```
import torch
tensor1 = torch.tensor([1, 2, 3])
tensor2 = torch.tensor([4, 5, 6])
result = tensor1 + tensor2
print(result)
```

Example Explanation:
- Adds corresponding elements of tensor1 and tensor2.
- Outputs: tensor([5, 7, 9])

2. Reduction Operation

What is a Reduction Operation?

Reduction operations compute a single value or a smaller tensor by aggregating elements of a tensor. Examples include summing, finding the maximum, or calculating the mean.

Syntax:
```
result = tensor.sum()
```

Detailed Explanation:
- **Purpose:** Aggregates tensor elements into a single value or along a specified dimension.
- **Parameters:**
  - dim (optional): Specifies the dimension to reduce. If omitted, the operation reduces all elements.
  - keepdim (optional): Retains reduced dimensions as singleton dimensions if set to True.
- **Behavior:** Reduction is performed efficiently using optimized algorithms.
- **Output:** A scalar or reduced tensor.

Example:
```
tensor = torch.tensor([[1, 2, 3], [4, 5, 6]])
result = tensor.sum(dim=0)
print(result)
```

Example Explanation:
- Computes the sum along dimension 0 (columns).
- Outputs: `tensor([5, 7, 9])`

3. Matrix Multiplication

What is Matrix Multiplication?
Matrix multiplication computes the dot product of rows and columns from two tensors. It is a core operation in linear algebra and neural networks.

Syntax:
```
result = torch.matmul(tensor1, tensor2)
```
Detailed Explanation:
- **Purpose:** Performs a linear transformation by multiplying two matrices.
- **Parameters:**
  - `tensor1, tensor2`: Input tensors where the inner dimensions must match.
- **Behavior:** Supports 2D matrix multiplication and batch matrix multiplication for higher dimensions.
- **Output:** A tensor containing the matrix product.

Example:
```
tensor1 = torch.tensor([[1, 2], [3, 4]])
tensor2 = torch.tensor([[5, 6], [7, 8]])
result = torch.matmul(tensor1, tensor2)
print(result)
```
Example Explanation:
- Multiplies two 2x2 tensors.
- Outputs: `tensor([[19, 22],`
  `        [43, 50]])`

4. Transpose
What is Transposing a Tensor?
Transposing a tensor swaps its dimensions, allowing for reorganization of data. This is often used in operations like reshaping data for matrix multiplication.

Syntax:
```
transposed = tensor.T
```

Detailed Explanation:

- **Purpose:** Reorganizes data by swapping rows and columns or other dimensions.
- **Parameters:**
  - `dim0`, `dim1`: Specifies dimensions to swap for higher-dimensional tensors (optional).
- **Behavior:**
  - For 2D tensors, T is equivalent to `transpose(0, 1)`.
  - For higher dimensions, specify dimensions explicitly.
- **Output:** A tensor with swapped dimensions.

Example:

```
tensor = torch.tensor([[1, 2, 3], [4, 5, 6]])
transposed = tensor.T
print(transposed)
```

Example Explanation:

- Transposes the 2x3 tensor to a 3x2 tensor.
- Outputs: `tensor([[1, 4],`
              `[2, 5],`
              `[3, 6]])`

5. In-place Addition

What is In-place Addition?

In-place addition modifies the original tensor directly by adding a specified value. This operation saves memory and reduces overhead.

Syntax:

```
tensor.add_(value)
```

Detailed Explanation:

- **Purpose:** Updates the tensor in place by adding a scalar value or another tensor.
- **Parameters:**
  - `value`: The scalar value or tensor to add.
- **Behavior:**
  - In-place operations are denoted by an underscore (e.g., `add_`).
  - The original tensor is modified, and no new tensor is created.
- **Output:** The modified tensor.

Example:
```
tensor = torch.tensor([1, 2, 3])
tensor.add_(5)
print(tensor)
```
Example Explanation:
- Adds 5 to each element of the tensor in place.
- Outputs: `tensor([6, 7, 8])`

Real-Life Project:

Project Name: Neural Network Input Normalization

Project Goal: Normalize input data for a neural network using tensor mathematical operations.

Code for This Project:
```
import torch
# Create a tensor of input data
inputs = torch.tensor([[2.0, 4.0], [6.0, 8.0]])
# Compute mean and standard deviation
mean = inputs.mean()
std = inputs.std()
# Normalize the input data
normalized_inputs = (inputs - mean) / std
print("Original Inputs:")
print(inputs)
print("\nNormalized Inputs:")
print(normalized_inputs)
```

Expected Output:
- **Original Inputs:**
```
tensor([[2.0, 4.0],
        [6.0, 8.0]])
```

- **Normalized Inputs:**
```
tensor([[-1.3416, -0.4472],
        [ 0.4472,  1.3416]])
```

Chapter -8 GPU Acceleration with PyTorch Tensors

GPU acceleration is a cornerstone of modern deep learning, enabling faster computation and efficient handling of large-scale data. PyTorch seamlessly integrates GPU acceleration, allowing users to perform tensor operations on GPUs with minimal code changes. This chapter explores the essentials of GPU acceleration using PyTorch tensors, including transferring data between CPU and GPU, performing operations on GPUs, and best practices.

Key Characteristics of GPU Acceleration in PyTorch:
- **Device Agnostic:** Code can run on both CPUs and GPUs with dynamic switching.
- **CUDA Integration:** Supports NVIDIA GPUs with CUDA for high-performance computations.
- **Tensor Operations:** Most PyTorch tensor operations are GPU-compatible.
- **Automatic Synchronization:** Ensures correct computation between CPU and GPU.
- **Scalability:** Efficiently handles large tensors and parallel computations.

Basic Rules for GPU Acceleration:
1. **CUDA Device:** Use `torch.device("cuda")` to specify GPU usage.
2. **Tensor Compatibility:** Tensors must be explicitly transferred to the GPU.
3. **Memory Management:** Monitor GPU memory usage to avoid out-of-memory errors.
4. **Device-Agnostic Code:** Use conditional checks to ensure compatibility with both CPU and GPU

Syntax Table:

SL No	Function	Syntax/Example	Description
1	Specify GPU Device	`device = torch.device("cuda")`	Defines the GPU as the computation device.
2	Transfer Tensor to GPU	`tensor = tensor.to(device)`	Moves a tensor to the specified device.
3	Perform Operations	`result = tensor1 + tensor2`	Executes tensor operations on the GPU.
4	Check CUDA Availability	`torch.cuda.is_available()`	Checks if CUDA is available on the system.
5	GPU Memory Management	`torch.cuda.memory_allocated()`	Monitors GPU memory usage.

Syntax Explanation:

1. Specify GPU Device

What is Specifying a GPU Device?

Specifying a GPU device ensures that all subsequent operations are executed on the GPU for accelerated performance.

Syntax:

`device = torch.device("cuda")`

Detailed Explanation:

- **Purpose:** Defines the target device (CPU or GPU) for tensor computations.
- **Parameters:**
    - `"cuda"`: Refers to the default GPU device (usually GPU 0).
    - `"cuda:<index>"`: Specifies a particular GPU if multiple GPUs are available (e.g., `"cuda:1"`).
    - `"cpu"`: Ensures computations are executed on the CPU.
- **Behavior:** Subsequent operations using tensors on this device will leverage the GPU for computation.

- **Output:** A device object specifying the computation target.

Example:

```
import torch
device = torch.device("cuda" if
torch.cuda.is_available() else "cpu")
print(device)
```

Example Explanation:

- Automatically selects the GPU if available; otherwise, falls back to the CPU.
- Outputs: cuda or cpu depending on system configuration.

2. Transfer Tensor to GPU

What is Transferring a Tensor to the GPU?

Transferring a tensor to the GPU makes it eligible for accelerated computations using CUDA.

Syntax:

```
tensor = tensor.to(device)
```

Detailed Explanation:

- **Purpose:** Moves tensor data from CPU memory to GPU memory for accelerated processing.
- **Parameters:**
  - device: The target device object (e.g., torch.device("cuda")).
- **Behavior:**
  - Creates a new tensor on the GPU with the same data and properties.
  - The original tensor remains on the CPU unless explicitly reassigned.
- **Output:** A new tensor residing on the specified device.

Example:

```
tensor = torch.tensor([1.0, 2.0, 3.0])
device = torch.device("cuda")
gpu_tensor = tensor.to(device)
print(gpu_tensor)
```

Example Explanation:

- Transfers the 1D tensor from CPU to GPU memory.
- Outputs: tensor([1., 2., 3.], device='cuda:0')

3. Perform Operations

What is Performing Operations on the GPU?

Tensor operations performed on GPU tensors leverage CUDA for faster execution, especially for large-scale computations.

Syntax:

```
result = tensor1 + tensor2
```

Detailed Explanation:

- **Purpose:** Executes mathematical or logical operations directly on GPU-resident tensors.
- **Parameters:**
    - tensor1, tensor2: Tensors located on the same device (GPU or CPU).
- **Behavior:**
    - Both tensors must reside on the same device; otherwise, PyTorch raises a runtime error.
    - Operations are optimized for parallel execution on the GPU.
- **Output:** A new tensor with the operation's result, residing on the GPU.

Example:

```
tensor1 = torch.tensor([1, 2, 3], device="cuda")
tensor2 = torch.tensor([4, 5, 6], device="cuda")
result = tensor1 + tensor2
print(result)
```

Example Explanation:

- Adds two tensors directly on the GPU.
- Outputs: tensor([5, 7, 9], device='cuda:0')

4. Check CUDA Availability

What is Checking CUDA Availability?

Checking CUDA availability ensures that the system has a compatible GPU and drivers for accelerated computations.

Syntax:

```
is_cuda_available = torch.cuda.is_available()
```

Detailed Explanation:

- **Purpose:** Confirms whether CUDA is installed and the GPU is accessible.

- **Behavior:**
  - ○ Returns `True` if a CUDA-capable GPU is detected and properly configured.
  - ○ Returns `False` otherwise.
- **Output:** A boolean value indicating CUDA availability.

Example:
```
if torch.cuda.is_available():
    print("CUDA is available.")
else:
    print("CUDA is not available.")
```
Example Explanation:

- Prints a message based on the availability of CUDA on the system.

5. GPU Memory Management

What is GPU Memory Management?

GPU memory management tracks and optimizes memory usage to avoid out-of-memory errors during tensor operations.

Syntax:
```
allocated_memory = torch.cuda.memory_allocated()
```
Detailed Explanation:

- **Purpose:** Monitors the amount of GPU memory currently in use by PyTorch tensors.
- **Behavior:**
  - ○ Reports memory usage in bytes.
  - ○ Helps identify memory bottlenecks in large-scale computations.
- **Output:** An integer representing allocated GPU memory in bytes.

Example:
```
tensor = torch.randn(1000, 1000, device="cuda")
memory_used = torch.cuda.memory_allocated()
print(f"Memory Allocated: {memory_used / 1e6} MB")
```
Example Explanation:

- Allocates a large tensor on the GPU and reports the memory usage.
- Outputs: Memory usage in megabytes (MB).

Real-Life Project:

Project Name: Accelerated Matrix Multiplication

Project Goal: Perform large-scale matrix multiplication using GPU acceleration.

Code for This Project:
```python
import torch
# Specify the device
device = torch.device("cuda" if
torch.cuda.is_available() else "cpu")
# Create large random matrices on the GPU
matrix1 = torch.randn(1000, 1000, device=device)
matrix2 = torch.randn(1000, 1000, device=device)
# Perform matrix multiplication
result = torch.matmul(matrix1, matrix2)
print("Matrix multiplication completed on:", device)
```

Expected Output:
- Confirms matrix multiplication is completed on the GPU if available.
- Demonstrates the significant speedup achieved with GPU acceleration for large-scale computations.

Chapter - 9 Building Your First Neural Network with PyTorch

This chapter provides a hands-on introduction to building and training a simple neural network using PyTorch. Neural networks are the foundation of deep learning, and PyTorch's dynamic computational graph makes creating and experimenting with models intuitive. This guide walks you through defining a model, specifying a loss function, choosing an optimizer, and training the network on a dataset.

Key Characteristics of Neural Networks in PyTorch:
- **Dynamic Computational Graph:** Enables flexibility in building models and debugging.
- **Modular Design:** PyTorch provides `torch.nn` for layers and models, `torch.optim` for optimizers, and `torch.utils.data` for data handling.
- **GPU Acceleration:** Seamlessly supports GPU for faster computations.
- **Customizability:** Allows defining custom layers, loss functions, and training loops.

Steps to Build a Neural Network:
1. **Prepare the Dataset:** Load and preprocess data using `torch.utils.data.DataLoader`.
2. **Define the Model:** Use `torch.nn.Module` to create the neural network architecture.
3. **Specify Loss Function:** Choose a loss function to quantify the error (e.g., `torch.nn.CrossEntropyLoss`).
4. **Choose Optimizer:** Select an optimization algorithm to update weights (e.g., `torch.optim.SGD`).
5. **Train the Model:** Implement a training loop to iteratively update weights using the optimizer and loss.
6. **Evaluate Performance:** Test the model's accuracy on unseen data.

Syntax Table:

SL No	Function	Syntax/Example	Description
1	Define Model Architecture	`class Model(nn.Module)`	Creates a custom neural network class.
2	Specify Loss Function	`criterion = nn.CrossEntropy Loss()`	Defines the loss function for classification tasks.
3	Choose Optimizer	`optimizer = optim.SGD(model .parameters(), lr=0.01)`	Specifies the optimization algorithm and learning rate.
4	Training Loop	`for epoch in range(epochs):`	Iterates over epochs and updates model weights.
5	Evaluate Model	`model.eval()`	Switches the model to evaluation mode.

Syntax Explanation:

1. Define Model Architecture

What is Model Definition?

Defining a model involves specifying the architecture of the neural network, including layers and forward pass logic. This step is essential as it determines how data flows through the network and how the model processes inputs to produce outputs.

Syntax:

```
import torch.nn as nn
class Model(nn.Module):
    def __init__(self):
        super(Model, self).__init__()
        self.layer1 = nn.Linear(784, 128)
        self.layer2 = nn.Linear(128, 10)
    def forward(self, x):
        x = torch.relu(self.layer1(x))
        x = self.layer2(x)
        return x
```

Detailed Explanation:

- **Purpose:** Defines the structure of the neural network, including input, hidden, and output layers.
- **Components:**
  - `__init__`: Initializes the layers of the model, specifying the number of inputs and outputs for each layer.
  - `forward`: Implements the forward pass logic, defining how data flows through the layers.
- **Output:** A custom model class inheriting from `nn.Module` that can be used for training and inference.
- **Behavior:** The model's `forward` method is automatically called during training or inference.

2. Specify Loss Function

What is a Loss Function?

A loss function quantifies the difference between the model's predictions and the true labels. It provides a scalar value that the optimization algorithm minimizes during training.

Syntax:

```
criterion = nn.CrossEntropyLoss()
```

Detailed Explanation:

- **Purpose:** Measures the error in classification tasks where outputs are probabilities (e.g., softmax outputs).
- **Parameters:**
  - `reduction`: Specifies how to aggregate the loss values (default is `mean`).
- **Output:** A loss value used to calculate gradients during backpropagation.
- **Behavior:** The loss function expects raw scores (logits) from the model's output layer and applies a combination of `softmax` and `negative log likelihood` internally.

3. Choose Optimizer

What is an Optimizer?

An optimizer updates the model's weights based on the gradients calculated during backpropagation, helping the model learn to minimize the loss function.

Syntax:

```
optimizer = torch.optim.SGD(model.parameters(),
lr=0.01)
```

Detailed Explanation:

- **Purpose:** Controls the learning process by adjusting weights to minimize the loss.
- **Parameters:**
    - `model.parameters()`: Specifies the model's trainable parameters to be updated.
    - `lr`: The learning rate, which determines the step size for updates.
- **Behavior:**
    - Updates weights using the selected optimization algorithm (e.g., SGD, Adam).
    - Allows setting additional parameters like momentum or weight decay.
- **Output:** An optimizer object that coordinates weight updates during training.

4. Training Loop

What is a Training Loop?

A training loop iteratively updates model weights over multiple epochs, using batches of data to optimize the loss function.

Syntax:

```
for epoch in range(epochs):
    for batch in dataloader:
        optimizer.zero_grad()
        outputs = model(inputs)
        loss = criterion(outputs, targets)
        loss.backward()
        optimizer.step()
```

Detailed Explanation:

- **Purpose:** Automates the process of training the model by iteratively refining weights.

- **Steps:**
  - `optimizer.zero_grad()`: Clears old gradients to prevent accumulation.
  - `loss.backward()`: Computes gradients of the loss with respect to model parameters.
  - `optimizer.step()`: Updates model weights using the computed gradients.
- **Behavior:** Processes the data in mini-batches for efficiency, allowing the model to learn incrementally.
- **Output:** Updated model weights after each epoch.

5. Evaluate Model

What is Model Evaluation?

Model evaluation assesses the trained model's performance on unseen data, ensuring it generalizes well to new inputs.

Syntax:

```
model.eval()
with torch.no_grad():
    predictions = model(inputs)
```

Detailed Explanation:

- **Purpose:** Tests the model without updating weights, providing an unbiased measure of performance.
- **Components:**
  - `model.eval()`: Switches the model to evaluation mode, disabling certain features like dropout.
  - `torch.no_grad()`: Temporarily disables gradient calculations to save memory and speed up computation.
- **Output:** Predictions or metrics like accuracy, precision, and recall.

Real-Life Project:

Project Name: Handwritten Digit Classification

Project Goal: Build and train a neural network to classify handwritten digits using the MNIST dataset.

Code for This Project:

```
import torch
import torch.nn as nn
import torch.optim as optim
from torchvision import datasets, transforms
```

```python
from torch.utils.data import DataLoader
# Load dataset
transform = transforms.ToTensor()
train_dataset = datasets.MNIST(root='data', train=True,
transform=transform, download=True)
train_loader = DataLoader(train_dataset, batch_size=64,
shuffle=True)
# Define model
class Model(nn.Module):
    def __init__(self):
        super(Model, self).__init__()
        self.layer1 = nn.Linear(28*28, 128)
        self.layer2 = nn.Linear(128, 10)
    def forward(self, x):
        x = x.view(x.size(0), -1)  # Flatten input
        x = torch.relu(self.layer1(x))
        x = self.layer2(x)
        return x
model = Model()
# Define loss function and optimizer
criterion = nn.CrossEntropyLoss()
optimizer = optim.SGD(model.parameters(), lr=0.01)
# Train the model
epochs = 5
for epoch in range(epochs):
    for images, labels in train_loader:
        optimizer.zero_grad()
        outputs = model(images)
        loss = criterion(outputs, labels)
        loss.backward()
        optimizer.step()
    print(f"Epoch {epoch+1}/{epochs}, Loss:
{loss.item():.4f}")
print("Training complete.")
```

Expected Output:

- Training loss decreases over epochs.
- Model is trained to classify digits effectively on the MNIST dataset.

Chapter - 10 PyTorch Modules and Layers

PyTorch modules and layers are the building blocks for creating and training deep learning models. PyTorch's `torch.nn` module provides pre-defined layers and a base class `nn.Module` to define custom models. This chapter explains the components of PyTorch modules, how to create and use layers, and the flexibility they offer for building neural networks.

Key Characteristics of PyTorch Modules and Layers:

- **Modularity:** Layers and modules are reusable and composable.
- **Customizability:** Define custom modules by extending the `nn.Module` class.
- **Layer Abstraction:** Simplifies handling weights, biases, and computations.
- **Integration:** Compatible with PyTorch's autograd and optimizers.
- **Support for Various Layers:** Includes fully connected, convolutional, recurrent, and normalization layers.

Steps to Use PyTorch Modules and Layers:

1. **Import `torch.nn`:** Access pre-defined layers and the `Module` base class.
2. **Define a Custom Module:** Extend `nn.Module` to create a neural network or subcomponent.
3. **Initialize Layers:** Use `nn.Linear`, `nn.Conv2d`, etc., in the `__init__` method.
4. **Implement Forward Pass:** Define how input tensors flow through the layers in the `forward` method.
5. **Use Layers in Training:** Integrate layers into a training loop for model optimization.

Syntax Table:

SL No	Function	Syntax/Example	Description
1	Define Custom Module	`class CustomModel(nn.Module)`	Creates a custom neural network class.
2	Fully Connected Layer	`nn.Linear(in_features, out_features)`	Creates a dense layer for processing inputs.
3	Convolutional Layer	`nn.Conv2d(in_channels, out_channels, kernel_size)`	Adds a convolutional layer for image data.
4	Activation Function	`torch.relu(input)`	Applies ReLU activation to tensor elements.
5	Sequential Module	`nn.Sequential(layers ...)`	Chains layers in a sequential model.

Syntax Explanation:

1. Define Custom Module

What is a Custom Module?

A custom module encapsulates the architecture of a neural network. It combines layers and forward pass logic to process input data, making it a reusable building block for deep learning models.

Syntax:

```
import torch.nn as nn
class CustomModel(nn.Module):
    def __init__(self):
        super(CustomModel, self).__init__()
        self.fc1 = nn.Linear(784, 128)  # Input to
first layer
        self.fc2 = nn.Linear(128, 10)   # Output layer
    def forward(self, x):
        x = torch.relu(self.fc1(x))
        x = self.fc2(x)
        return x
```

Detailed Explanation:

- **Purpose:** Encapsulates the structure of a neural network by defining layers and their interconnections.
- **Components:**
  - __init__: Initializes the layers as attributes of the module. Each layer represents a transformation in the model.
  - forward: Defines how data flows through the network during the forward pass. This method must be implemented for all nn.Module subclasses.
- **Behavior:**
  - The module handles parameter registration, gradient computation, and forward propagation seamlessly.
  - forward logic can include complex combinations of layers, activations, and custom operations.
- **Output:** Returns the result of passing the input through the defined layers.

2. Fully Connected Layer
What is a Fully Connected Layer?
A fully connected (dense) layer connects every input feature to every output neuron. It is commonly used in feedforward neural networks for tasks like classification and regression.
Syntax:
```
layer = nn.Linear(in_features, out_features)
```
Detailed Explanation:

- **Purpose:** Applies a linear transformation to the input, producing weighted sums of inputs for each output neuron.
- **Parameters:**
  - in_features: Number of input features (e.g., the size of a flattened image).
  - out_features: Number of output features (e.g., the number of classes in a classification problem).
- **Behavior:**
  - During training, the layer learns weights and biases to map inputs to outputs.

o Performs the operation: `output = input @ weight.T + bias`.
- **Output:** A tensor with shape `[batch_size, out_features]`.

3. Convolutional Layer
What is a Convolutional Layer?
A convolutional layer extracts spatial features from input data by applying learnable filters, making it essential for image and video processing tasks.

Syntax:
```
conv = nn.Conv2d(in_channels, out_channels, kernel_size)
```

Detailed Explanation:
- **Purpose:** Detects patterns such as edges, textures, or shapes in input images.
- **Parameters:**
    o `in_channels`: Number of input channels (e.g., 1 for grayscale images, 3 for RGB images).
    o `out_channels`: Number of filters to apply, each producing a feature map.
    o `kernel_size`: Size of the convolution filter (e.g., 3 for a 3x3 filter).
    o Optional parameters include `stride`, `padding`, and `dilation`, which control the filter's movement and output size.
- **Behavior:**
    o Slides the filter over the input tensor, performing element-wise multiplications and summing results.
    o Outputs feature maps that highlight specific characteristics of the input.
- **Output:** A tensor of feature maps with reduced or same spatial dimensions, depending on the stride and padding.

4. Activation Function
What is an Activation Function?
An activation function introduces non-linearity into the model, enabling it to learn complex patterns and relationships in the data.

Syntax:

```
output = torch.relu(input)
```

Detailed Explanation:

- **Purpose:** Transforms the output of a layer to add non-linearity, allowing the network to model complex relationships.
- **Common Functions:**
  - `torch.relu`: ReLU (Rectified Linear Unit), sets negative values to 0.
  - `torch.sigmoid`: Maps values to a range between 0 and 1.
  - `torch.tanh`: Maps values to a range between -1 and 1.
- **Behavior:**
  - Processes each element independently.
  - Prevents the network from collapsing into a simple linear model.
- **Output:** A tensor with the same shape as the input, with transformed values.

5. Sequential Module

What is a Sequential Module?

A sequential module simplifies the definition of linear models by chaining multiple layers and operations in sequence.

Syntax:

```
model = nn.Sequential(
    nn.Linear(784, 128),
    nn.ReLU(),
    nn.Linear(128, 10)
)
```

Detailed Explanation:

- **Purpose:** Provides a compact way to stack layers and activations for simple feedforward architectures.
- **Parameters:**
  - `layers...`: A sequence of `nn.Module` layers and activation functions.
- **Behavior:**
  - Passes the input through each layer in the defined order.
  - Eliminates the need for a custom `forward` method for

simple models.

- **Output:** A model object that can process input tensors end-to-end.

Real-Life Project:
Project Name: Image Classification Using Predefined Layers
Project Goal: Build a neural network to classify images from the CIFAR-10 dataset using convolutional and fully connected layers.
Code for This Project:

```python
import torch
import torch.nn as nn
import torch.optim as optim
from torchvision import datasets, transforms
from torch.utils.data import DataLoader

# Data preprocessing
transform = transforms.Compose([
    transforms.ToTensor(),
    transforms.Normalize((0.5,), (0.5,))
])
train_dataset = datasets.CIFAR10(root='data',
train=True, transform=transform, download=True)
train_loader = DataLoader(train_dataset, batch_size=64,
shuffle=True)

# Define the model
class CIFAR10Model(nn.Module):
    def __init__(self):
        super(CIFAR10Model, self).__init__()
        self.conv1 = nn.Conv2d(3, 16, 3, padding=1)  #
3 input channels, 16 filters
        self.conv2 = nn.Conv2d(16, 32, 3, padding=1)
        self.fc1 = nn.Linear(32 * 8 * 8, 128)  #
Flattened input from 32 feature maps
        self.fc2 = nn.Linear(128, 10)
```

```python
    def forward(self, x):
        x = torch.relu(self.conv1(x))
        x = torch.relu(self.conv2(x))
        x = torch.flatten(x, 1)  # Flatten for fully
connected layers
        x = torch.relu(self.fc1(x))
        x = self.fc2(x)
        return x

model = CIFAR10Model()

# Define loss and optimizer
criterion = nn.CrossEntropyLoss()
optimizer = optim.Adam(model.parameters(), lr=0.001)

# Training loop
epochs = 5
for epoch in range(epochs):
    for images, labels in train_loader:
        optimizer.zero_grad()
        outputs = model(images)
        loss = criterion(outputs, labels)
        loss.backward()
        optimizer.step()
    print(f"Epoch {epoch+1}/{epochs}, Loss:
{loss.item():.4f}")

print("Training complete.")
```

Expected Output:
- Training loss decreases over epochs.
- The model learns to classify images into 10 classes using convolutional layers and fully connected layers.

Chapter - 11 Using the Sequential API for Simple Models

The Sequential API in PyTorch provides a streamlined way to define simple neural network architectures. This API is particularly suitable for feedforward networks, where layers are arranged in a linear sequence. It allows users to define and connect layers and activations without explicitly writing a forward method. This chapter explores the usage of the Sequential API to create efficient and readable models.

Key Characteristics of the Sequential API:

- **Simplicity:** Simplifies the definition of models with a linear stack of layers.
- **Readability:** Provides a concise way to organize layers and operations.
- **Flexibility:** Allows the inclusion of pre-defined and custom layers.
- **Interoperability:** Seamlessly integrates with PyTorch's autograd and optimizers.
- **Debugging:** Facilitates easier debugging for straightforward architectures.

Steps to Use the Sequential API:

1. **Import torch.nn:** Access the nn.Sequential module and predefined layers.
2. **Define the Model:** Use nn.Sequential to stack layers in order.
3. **Add Layers and Activations:** Specify layers and activations directly in the constructor.
4. **Train the Model:** Use the model in training loops as you would with any PyTorch model.

Syntax Table:

SL No	Function	Syntax/Example	Description
1	Create Sequential Model	`model = nn.Sequential(la yers...)`	Defines a model by stacking layers in sequence.
2	Add Fully Connected Layer	`nn.Linear(in_fea tures, out_features)`	Adds a dense layer to the model.
3	Add Activation Function	`nn.ReLU()`	Introduces non-linearity into the model.
4	Combine Operations	`nn.Sequential(nn .Linear(), nn.ReLU())`	Combines layers and activations.
5	Forward Pass	`outputs = model(inputs)`	Passes data through the sequential model.

Syntax Explanation:

1. Create Sequential Model

What is a Sequential Model?

A Sequential model organizes layers in a linear stack, where each layer feeds its output to the next layer as input. It eliminates the need for explicitly writing a forward method.

Syntax:

```
model = nn.Sequential(
    nn.Linear(784, 128),
    nn.ReLU(),
    nn.Linear(128, 10)
)
```

Detailed Explanation:

- **Purpose:** Simplifies the creation of linear models for tasks like classification and regression.
- **Parameters:**
    - `layers...`: A sequence of nn.Module layers and

activation functions.

- **Behavior:**
  - ○ Layers are executed in the order they are defined.
  - ○ Data flows sequentially through the specified layers without needing a custom `forward` method.
- **Output:** A model object capable of processing input tensors.

Example:

```
model = nn.Sequential(
    nn.Linear(28 * 28, 128),
    nn.ReLU(),
    nn.Linear(128, 10)
)
print(model)
```

Example Explanation:

- Defines a model with an input layer, hidden layer, and output layer.
- Outputs the model architecture as a readable string, showing the layers and their parameters.

2. Add Fully Connected Layer

What is Adding a Fully Connected Layer?

A fully connected layer transforms input features into output features by learning weights and biases during training.

Syntax:

```
nn.Linear(in_features, out_features)
```

Detailed Explanation:

- **Purpose:** Implements a linear transformation, producing weighted sums for each output feature.
- **Parameters:**
  - ○ `in_features`: Number of input features (e.g., flattened image size).
  - ○ `out_features`: Number of output features (e.g., classes).
- **Behavior:**
  - ○ Multiplies input tensors with a weight matrix and adds biases.

o   Learns weights and biases through backpropagation.
- **Output:** A transformed tensor with shape [batch_size, out_features].

Example:
```
layer = nn.Linear(128, 64)
data = torch.randn(32, 128)  # Batch of 32 samples with
128 features each
output = layer(data)
print(output.shape)
```
Example Explanation:
- Defines a fully connected layer mapping 128 input features to 64 output features.
- Processes a batch of 32 samples and produces an output of shape [32, 64].

3. Add Activation Function
What is Adding an Activation Function?
Activation functions introduce non-linearity into the model, enabling it to learn complex patterns in the data.
Syntax:
```
nn.ReLU()
```
Detailed Explanation:
- **Purpose:** Applies non-linear transformations to the outputs of preceding layers.
- **Common Activations:**
  o   nn.ReLU(): Rectified Linear Unit, sets negative values to zero.
  o   nn.Sigmoid(): Maps values to the range [0, 1].
  o   nn.Tanh(): Maps values to the range [-1, 1].
- **Behavior:**
  o   Processes each element of the input tensor independently.
  o   Ensures the network can approximate non-linear relationships.
- **Output:** A tensor with the same shape as the input but transformed values.

Example:

```
activation = nn.ReLU()
data = torch.tensor([[-1.0, 2.0], [0.0, -3.0]])
output = activation(data)
print(output)
```

Example Explanation:

- Applies the ReLU function to a 2x2 tensor.
- Sets all negative values to zero, producing `tensor([[0.0, 2.0], [0.0, 0.0]])`.

4. Combine Operations

What is Combining Operations?

Combining operations stacks layers and activations in sequence to build a complete model.

Syntax:

```
nn.Sequential(
    nn.Linear(784, 128),
    nn.ReLU(),
    nn.Linear(128, 10)
)
```

Detailed Explanation:

- **Purpose:** Builds a complete neural network model by chaining multiple operations.
- **Parameters:**
  - `layers...`: A sequence of layers and functions to apply sequentially.
- **Behavior:**
  - Automatically connects the output of one layer to the input of the next.
  - Eliminates the need for manually defining data flow logic.
- **Output:** A unified model that combines all specified layers and activations.

Example:

```
model = nn.Sequential(
    nn.Linear(784, 128),
    nn.ReLU(),
```

```
    nn.Linear(128, 64),
    nn.ReLU(),
    nn.Linear(64, 10)
)
data = torch.randn(32, 784)
output = model(data)
print(output.shape)
```
Example Explanation:

- Creates a model with three layers and two activation functions.
- Processes a batch of 32 samples with 784 features each and produces an output of shape [32, 10].

5. Forward Pass

What is a Forward Pass?

The forward pass feeds input data through the model to produce outputs. In a sequential model, this happens implicitly when calling the model object.

Syntax:
```
outputs = model(inputs)
```
Detailed Explanation:

- **Purpose:** Processes input tensors through the sequentially defined layers to generate predictions or intermediate outputs.
- **Parameters:**
    - inputs: A tensor containing the data to process.
- **Behavior:**
    - The model automatically applies each layer in sequence.
    - Computes intermediate and final outputs without requiring explicit forward pass logic.
- **Output:** A tensor containing the model's predictions or transformed data.

Example:
```
data = torch.randn(64, 784)  # Batch of 64 samples
outputs = model(data)
print(outputs)
```
Example Explanation:

- Passes a batch of 64 samples through the sequential model.

- Outputs a tensor with predictions, typically of shape [64, 10] for a 10-class problem.

Real-Life Project:
Project Name: Simple Digit Classifier with Sequential API
Project Goal: Build and train a simple feedforward neural network to classify handwritten digits from the MNIST dataset using the Sequential API.
Code for This Project:

```
import torch
import torch.nn as nn
import torch.optim as optim
from torchvision import datasets, transforms
from torch.utils.data import DataLoader


# Data preprocessing
transform = transforms.ToTensor()
train_dataset = datasets.MNIST(root='data', train=True,
transform=transform, download=True)
train_loader = DataLoader(train_dataset, batch_size=64,
shuffle=True)


# Define the model using Sequential API
model = nn.Sequential(
    nn.Linear(28*28, 128),   # Input layer
    nn.ReLU(),               # Activation
    nn.Linear(128, 64),      # Hidden layer
    nn.ReLU(),               # Activation
    nn.Linear(64, 10)        # Output layer
)


# Define loss function and optimizer
criterion = nn.CrossEntropyLoss()
optimizer = optim.SGD(model.parameters(), lr=0.01)


# Training loop
epochs = 5
```

```
for epoch in range(epochs):
    for images, labels in train_loader:
        images = images.view(images.size(0), -1)  #
Flatten the images
        optimizer.zero_grad()
        outputs = model(images)
        loss = criterion(outputs, labels)
        loss.backward()
        optimizer.step()
    print(f"Epoch {epoch+1}/{epochs}, Loss:
{loss.item():.4f}")

print("Training complete.")
```

Expected Output:

- Training loss decreases over epochs.
- The model learns to classify digits effectively using the Sequential API.

Chapter - 12 Building Custom Layers and Models

Building custom layers and models in PyTorch empowers developers to design neural networks tailored to specific tasks and requirements. While PyTorch provides a variety of pre-defined layers and models, custom implementations offer greater flexibility and enable innovative solutions. This chapter explores how to define custom layers and models by extending PyTorch's nn.Module class.

Key Characteristics of Custom Layers and Models

- **Flexibility:** Provides full control over layer operations and model behavior.
- **Reusability:** Custom layers can be reused across multiple models.
- **Integration:** Seamlessly integrates with PyTorch's autograd and optimizers.
- **Innovation:** Enables the development of unique architectures for specific tasks.

Steps to Create Custom Layers and Models

1. **Define a Custom Layer:** Extend nn.Module and implement the desired functionality.
2. **Implement Forward Pass:** Define how input data flows through the layer.
3. **Create a Custom Model:** Combine standard and custom layers into a complete model.
4. **Train the Model:** Use the custom model in a typical training loop.

Syntax Table

SL No	Function	Syntax/Example	Description
1	Define Custom Layer	`class CustomLayer(nn.Module)`	Creates a layer with custom operations.
2	Implement Forward Pass	`def forward(self, input):`	Specifies the computation for the layer.
3	Combine Layers into Model	`class CustomModel(nn.Module)`	Builds a model using standard and custom layers.
4	Use Custom Layer	`self.custom_layer = CustomLayer()`	Integrates a custom layer into a model.
5	Train the Model	`outputs = model(inputs)`	Uses the model in a training loop.

Syntax Explanation

1. Define Custom Layer
What is a Custom Layer?

A custom layer encapsulates specific operations, enabling the creation of unique neural network components. It is defined by extending PyTorch's `nn.Module` class.

Syntax:

```
import torch.nn as nn
class CustomLayer(nn.Module):
    def __init__(self, input_dim, output_dim):
        super(CustomLayer, self).__init__()
        self.weight =
nn.Parameter(torch.randn(input_dim, output_dim))
    def forward(self, x):
        return torch.matmul(x, self.weight)
```

Detailed Explanation:

- **Purpose:** Encapsulates a specific operation or transformation for reuse in models.

- **Components:**
  - __init__: Initializes parameters or submodules needed for the layer.
  - forward: Defines how the layer processes input data.
- **Output:** A custom layer object that can be integrated into a model.

Example:
```
layer = CustomLayer(4, 2)
data = torch.randn(3, 4)  # Batch of 3 samples with 4
features each
output = layer(data)
print(output)
```
Example Explanation:

- Creates a custom layer with 4 input features and 2 output features.
- Processes a batch of 3 samples and returns the transformed data.

2. Implement Forward Pass
What is a Forward Pass?
The forward pass defines the computations performed by a layer or model when processing input data.
Syntax:
```
def forward(self, input):
    return output
```
Detailed Explanation:

- **Purpose:** Specifies the transformation applied to the input tensor.
- **Parameters:**
  - input: The input tensor for the layer.
- **Behavior:**
  - Executes operations on the input tensor.
  - Can include pre-defined layers, custom operations, or both.
- **Output:** The transformed tensor after applying the forward pass logic.

Example:
```
class CustomLayer(nn.Module):
    def __init__(self, input_dim, output_dim):
        super(CustomLayer, self).__init__()
        self.linear = nn.Linear(input_dim, output_dim)
    def forward(self, x):
        return torch.relu(self.linear(x))
layer = CustomLayer(4, 2)
data = torch.randn(3, 4)
output = layer(data)
print(output)
```
Example Explanation:
- Combines a linear transformation and ReLU activation in the forward pass.
- Processes input data and outputs the transformed tensor.

3. Combine Layers into Model
What is Combining Layers into a Model?
Combining layers into a model organizes the neural network structure, defining how data flows through multiple components.
Syntax:
```
class CustomModel(nn.Module):
    def __init__(self):
        super(CustomModel, self).__init__()
        self.layer1 = nn.Linear(4, 8)
        self.custom_layer = CustomLayer(8, 2)
    def forward(self, x):
        x = torch.relu(self.layer1(x))
        return self.custom_layer(x)
```
Detailed Explanation:
- **Purpose:** Creates a reusable model that integrates standard and custom layers.
- **Components:**
  - __init__: Initializes layers as attributes.
  - forward: Specifies how data flows through the model.
- **Output:** A complete model ready for training and inference.

Example:
```
model = CustomModel()
data = torch.randn(5, 4)  # Batch of 5 samples with 4
features each
output = model(data)
print(output)
```
Example Explanation:
- Defines a model with a standard linear layer and a custom layer.
- Processes a batch of input data and outputs the result.

4. Use Custom Layer
What is Using a Custom Layer?
Using a custom layer integrates its unique functionality into a larger model.
Syntax:
```
self.custom_layer = CustomLayer()
```
Detailed Explanation:
- **Purpose:** Embeds the custom layer into a model for use during training and inference.
- **Behavior:**
  - Calls the custom layer's forward method during the model's forward pass.
  - Enables modular design and reuse of custom layers.
- **Output:** Transformed data after processing by the custom layer.

Example:
```
class CustomModel(nn.Module):
    def __init__(self):
        super(CustomModel, self).__init__()
        self.custom_layer = CustomLayer(4, 2)

    def forward(self, x):
        return self.custom_layer(x)
model = CustomModel()
data = torch.randn(3, 4)
output = model(data)
print(output)
```

Example Explanation:
- Integrates a custom layer directly into the model.
- Processes input data using the custom layer's logic.

5. Train the Model
What is Training the Model?
Training a model optimizes its parameters using data, a loss function, and an optimization algorithm.
Syntax:
```
outputs = model(inputs)
```
Detailed Explanation:
- **Purpose:** Processes input data to compute predictions during training.
- **Steps:**
  - Perform a forward pass through the model.
  - Compute the loss between predictions and true labels.
  - Backpropagate gradients and update weights.
- **Output:** Predictions or intermediate outputs during training.

Example:
```
model = CustomModel()
data = torch.randn(10, 4)
labels = torch.randint(0, 2, (10,))
criterion = nn.CrossEntropyLoss()
optimizer = torch.optim.SGD(model.parameters(),
lr=0.01)
for epoch in range(5):
    optimizer.zero_grad()
    outputs = model(data)
    loss = criterion(outputs, labels)
    loss.backward()
    optimizer.step()
    print(f"Epoch {epoch+1}, Loss: {loss.item():.4f}")
```
Example Explanation:
- Trains the model using a batch of data and updates its parameters.
- Prints the loss after each epoch, showing the model's

improvement.

Real-Life Project

Project Name: Custom Layer-Based Sentiment Classifier
Project Goal: Build and train a sentiment classifier using a custom embedding layer and a feedforward neural network.

Code for This Project:

```python
import torch
import torch.nn as nn
import torch.optim as optim

# Custom Embedding Layer
class CustomEmbeddingLayer(nn.Module):
    def __init__(self, vocab_size, embed_dim):
        super(CustomEmbeddingLayer, self).__init__()
        self.embedding = nn.Embedding(vocab_size, embed_dim)

    def forward(self, x):
        return self.embedding(x)


# Sentiment Classifier
class SentimentClassifier(nn.Module):
    def __init__(self, vocab_size, embed_dim, hidden_dim, output_dim):
        super(SentimentClassifier, self).__init__()
        self.embedding = CustomEmbeddingLayer(vocab_size, embed_dim)
        self.fc1 = nn.Linear(embed_dim, hidden_dim)
        self.fc2 = nn.Linear(hidden_dim, output_dim)

    def forward(self, x):
        x = self.embedding(x).mean(dim=1)  # Average embedding
        x = torch.relu(self.fc1(x))
```

```python
        return self.fc2(x)
# Model, Loss, Optimizer
vocab_size = 10000
model = SentimentClassifier(vocab_size, embed_dim=50,
hidden_dim=128, output_dim=2)
criterion = nn.CrossEntropyLoss()
optimizer = optim.Adam(model.parameters(), lr=0.001)

# Dummy Data
inputs = torch.randint(0, vocab_size, (32, 100))  #
Batch of 32 samples, each with 100 tokens
labels = torch.randint(0, 2, (32,))

# Training Loop
for epoch in range(5):
    optimizer.zero_grad()
    outputs = model(inputs)
    loss = criterion(outputs, labels)
    loss.backward()
    optimizer.step()
    print(f"Epoch {epoch+1}, Loss: {loss.item():.4f}")
```
Expected Output:
- Training loss decreases over epochs.
- Model learns to classify sentiment effectively using custom embedding and linear layers.

Chapter - 13 Forward and Backward Pass

The forward and backward passes are fundamental components of training a neural network in PyTorch. The forward pass computes the output of the network given the input, while the backward pass calculates the gradients needed to update the model's parameters during optimization. This chapter explains how these processes work, including their role in training and how PyTorch automates much of the complexity.

Key Characteristics of Forward and Backward Passes

- **Forward Pass:** Propagates input through the network to produce outputs.
- **Backward Pass:** Computes gradients for each parameter using backpropagation.
- **Automatic Differentiation:** PyTorch's autograd simplifies gradient computation.
- **Integration:** Forward and backward passes seamlessly integrate with optimizers.
- **Efficiency:** Optimized for GPU acceleration.

Steps in Forward and Backward Passes

1. **Perform Forward Pass:** Calculate model predictions using the input data.
2. **Compute Loss:** Measure the difference between predictions and true labels.
3. **Execute Backward Pass:** Calculate gradients for all trainable parameters.
4. **Update Parameters:** Use an optimizer to adjust model weights.

Syntax Table

SL No	Function	Syntax/Example	Description
1	Perform Forward Pass	`outputs = model(inputs)`	Computes predictions from input data.
2	Compute Loss	`loss = criterion(outputs, targets)`	Calculates the loss between predictions and labels.
3	Zero Gradients	`optimizer.zero_grad()`	Clears old gradients to avoid accumulation.
4	Execute Backward Pass	`loss.backward()`	Computes gradients via backpropagation.
5	Update Parameters	`optimizer.step()`	Adjusts model weights using the gradients.

Syntax Explanation

1. Perform Forward Pass
What is a Forward Pass?
The forward pass propagates input data through the network, layer by layer, to compute predictions or intermediate outputs.
Syntax:
`outputs = model(inputs)`
Detailed Explanation:
- **Purpose:** Computes the model's predictions for the given inputs.
- **Parameters:**
  - `inputs`: The input tensor fed to the model.
- **Behavior:**
  - Applies all layers and operations defined in the model's forward method.
  - Outputs predictions or intermediate tensors based on the architecture.
- **Output:** A tensor containing the model's predictions.

Example:

```
outputs = model(torch.randn(64, 784))   # Batch of 64
samples, each with 784 features
print(outputs.shape)
```

Example Explanation:

- Processes a batch of input data through the model.
- Outputs predictions, typically matching the shape of the target labels.

2. Compute Loss

What is Loss Computation?

Loss computation measures the error between the model's predictions and the true labels, guiding the optimization process.

Syntax:

```
loss = criterion(outputs, targets)
```

Detailed Explanation:

- **Purpose:** Provides a scalar value representing the model's prediction error.
- **Parameters:**
  - `outputs`: Predictions from the forward pass.
  - `targets`: Ground-truth labels.
- **Behavior:**
  - Computes the difference between predictions and true labels.
  - Supports various loss functions like MSE, CrossEntropy, etc.
- **Output:** A scalar tensor representing the loss.

Example:

```
criterion = nn.CrossEntropyLoss()
loss = criterion(outputs, torch.randint(0, 10, (64,)))
# Batch of 64 labels
print(loss.item())
```

Example Explanation:

- Computes the cross-entropy loss for a batch of predictions and labels.
- Outputs a single scalar value indicating the error.

3. Zero Gradients
What is Zeroing Gradients?
Zeroing gradients ensures that gradients from the previous iteration do not accumulate during backpropagation.
Syntax:
```
optimizer.zero_grad()
```
Detailed Explanation:
- **Purpose:** Clears the gradient buffers for all parameters before computing new gradients.
- **Behavior:**
  - Prevents gradients from adding up across multiple backward passes.
  - Ensures each training step uses only the gradients from the current iteration.
- **Output:** Clears gradients; no tensor is returned.

Example:
```
optimizer.zero_grad()
```
Example Explanation:
- Prepares the model for a new round of gradient computation.
- Ensures gradients from previous steps do not interfere.

4. Execute Backward Pass
What is a Backward Pass?
The backward pass computes gradients for each trainable parameter in the model using the chain rule of differentiation.
Syntax:
```
loss.backward()
```
Detailed Explanation:
- **Purpose:** Calculates the gradients of the loss with respect to all trainable parameters.
- **Behavior:**
  - Traverses the computation graph built during the forward pass.
  - Computes partial derivatives for each parameter.
- **Output:** Populates the .grad attribute of each parameter with its

gradient.

Example:
```
loss.backward()
```
Example Explanation:

- Executes backpropagation, computing gradients for all parameters.
- Gradients are stored in each parameter's `.grad` attribute.

5. Update Parameters
What is Updating Parameters?
Parameter updates adjust the model's weights based on the computed gradients and the optimizer's algorithm.

Syntax:
```
optimizer.step()
```
Detailed Explanation:

- **Purpose:** Applies the computed gradients to update the model's parameters.
- **Behavior:**
  - Uses the optimizer's algorithm (e.g., SGD, Adam) to modify weights.
  - Considers learning rate and optional hyperparameters like momentum.
- **Output:** Updates weights in place; no tensor is returned.

Example:
```
optimizer.step()
```
Example Explanation:

- Updates model parameters using the gradients computed in the backward pass.

Real-Life Project

Project Name: Training a Simple Feedforward Network
Project Goal: Build and train a neural network on the MNIST dataset using forward and backward passes.
Code for This Project:
```
import torch
```

```python
import torch.nn as nn
import torch.optim as optim
from torchvision import datasets, transforms
from torch.utils.data import DataLoader

# Data preprocessing
transform = transforms.ToTensor()
train_dataset = datasets.MNIST(root='data', train=True,
transform=transform, download=True)
train_loader = DataLoader(train_dataset, batch_size=64,
shuffle=True)

# Define the model
model = nn.Sequential(
    nn.Linear(28*28, 128),
    nn.ReLU(),
    nn.Linear(128, 64),
    nn.ReLU(),
    nn.Linear(64, 10)
)
# Define loss function and optimizer
criterion = nn.CrossEntropyLoss()
optimizer = optim.SGD(model.parameters(), lr=0.01)

# Training loop
epochs = 5
for epoch in range(epochs):
    for images, labels in train_loader:
        images = images.view(images.size(0), -1)  #
Flatten the images
        optimizer.zero_grad()  # Zero gradients
        outputs = model(images)  # Forward pass
        loss = criterion(outputs, labels)  # Compute
loss
        loss.backward()  # Backward pass
        optimizer.step()  # Update parameters
    print(f"Epoch {epoch+1}/{epochs}, Loss:
```

```
{loss.item():.4f}")
print("Training complete.")
```

Expected Output:

- Training loss decreases over epochs.
- Model learns to classify digits effectively using forward and backward passes.

Chapter - 14 Implementing Activation Functions in PyTorch

Activation functions are essential components of neural networks, introducing non-linearity to enable models to learn complex patterns. PyTorch provides a wide range of pre-defined activation functions in the `torch.nn` module, as well as operations in `torch` for custom implementations. This chapter explores the implementation and usage of activation functions in PyTorch, including their purpose, common types, and how to apply them in models.

Key Characteristics of Activation Functions

- **Non-linearity:** Allows models to capture complex relationships between inputs and outputs.
- **Modularity:** Easily integrated into PyTorch models as layers or functions.
- **Variety:** Includes widely used functions like ReLU, Sigmoid, and Tanh.
- **Customizability:** Enables the creation of custom activation functions.
- **Efficiency:** Optimized for GPU acceleration.

Steps to Use Activation Functions in PyTorch

1. **Choose an Activation Function:** Select a pre-defined or custom activation function.
2. **Apply Activation:** Use the function as part of the forward pass in the model.
3. **Integrate into Models:** Combine activation functions with layers in sequential or custom models.

Syntax Table

SL No	Function	Syntax/Example	Description
1	ReLU Activation	`torch.relu(input)`	Applies Rectified Linear Unit to the input.
2	Sigmoid Activation	`torch.sigmoid(input)`	Maps input values to the range [0, 1].
3	Tanh Activation	`torch.tanh(input)`	Maps input values to the range [-1, 1].
4	Pre-defined Layer Activation	`nn.ReLU()`	Adds activation as a layer in the model.
5	Custom Activation Function	`custom_function(input)`	Implements a user-defined activation function.

Syntax Explanation

1. ReLU Activation
What is ReLU?
Rectified Linear Unit (ReLU) is the most commonly used activation function, setting all negative values to zero while keeping positive values unchanged.
Syntax:
`output = torch.relu(input)`
Detailed Explanation:
- **Purpose:** Introduces non-linearity by zeroing out negative values.
- **Parameters:**
  - input: A tensor containing the input data.
- **Behavior:**
  - Processes each element of the tensor independently.
  - Retains computational simplicity and efficiency.
- **Output:** A tensor with the same shape as the input, with non-negative values.

Example:
```
import torch
input = torch.tensor([[-1.0, 2.0], [0.0, -3.0]])
output = torch.relu(input)
print(output)
```
Example Explanation:
- Input tensor `[[ -1.0, 2.0], [ 0.0, -3.0 ]]` is transformed to `[[ 0.0, 2.0], [ 0.0, 0.0 ]]` by setting all negative values to zero.

2. Sigmoid Activation
What is Sigmoid?
The sigmoid function maps input values to a range between 0 and 1, making it useful for binary classification tasks.
Syntax:
```
output = torch.sigmoid(input)
```
Detailed Explanation:
- **Purpose:** Scales input values to probabilities.
- **Parameters:**
  - input: A tensor containing the input data.
- **Behavior:**
  - Applies the sigmoid formula: `1 / (1 + exp(-x))`.
  - Compresses large positive values close to 1 and large negative values close to 0.
- **Output:** A tensor with the same shape as the input, containing values in [0, 1].

Example:
```
input = torch.tensor([[-1.0, 2.0], [0.0, -3.0]])
output = torch.sigmoid(input)
print(output)
```
Example Explanation:
- Input tensor `[[ -1.0, 2.0], [ 0.0, -3.0 ]]` is transformed to values between 0 and 1.

3. Tanh Activation
What is Tanh?
The Tanh (Hyperbolic Tangent) function maps input values to a range between -1 and 1, centering outputs around 0.

Syntax:
```
output = torch.tanh(input)
```

Detailed Explanation:
- **Purpose:** Provides non-linearity with centered outputs, often used in hidden layers.
- **Parameters:**
  - `input`: A tensor containing the input data.
- **Behavior:**
  - Applies the tanh formula: `(exp(x) - exp(-x)) / (exp(x) + exp(-x))`.
  - Compresses large positive values close to 1 and large negative values close to -1.
- **Output:** A tensor with the same shape as the input, containing values in [-1, 1].

Example:
```
input = torch.tensor([[-1.0, 2.0], [0.0, -3.0]])
output = torch.tanh(input)
print(output)
```

Example Explanation:
- Input tensor `[[ -1.0, 2.0], [ 0.0, -3.0 ]]` is transformed to values between -1 and 1.

4. Pre-defined Layer Activation
What is a Pre-defined Layer Activation?
Pre-defined activation layers, such as `nn.ReLU`, allow seamless integration of activation functions into models.

Syntax:
```
activation = nn.ReLU()
output = activation(input)
```

Detailed Explanation:
- **Purpose:** Embeds activation functions as reusable layers in models.

- **Parameters:**
  - input: A tensor containing the input data.
- **Behavior:**
  - Performs the same operations as functional equivalents like `torch.relu`.
  - Compatible with sequential and custom models.
- **Output:** A tensor with transformed values.

Example:
```
activation = nn.ReLU()
input = torch.tensor([[-1.0, 2.0], [0.0, -3.0]])
output = activation(input)
print(output)
```
Example Explanation:
- Uses `nn.ReLU` to transform the input tensor by setting negative values to zero.

5. Custom Activation Function
What is a Custom Activation Function?
A custom activation function implements user-defined operations for specialized tasks.
Syntax:
```
def custom_activation(input):
    return torch.max(input, torch.tensor(0.1))
```
Detailed Explanation:
- **Purpose:** Provides flexibility for unique requirements not met by standard functions.
- **Parameters:**
  - input: A tensor containing the input data.
- **Behavior:**
  - Executes a user-defined transformation on the input tensor.
- **Output:** A tensor with custom-transformed values.

Example:
```
def leaky_relu(input):
    return torch.where(input > 0, input, 0.01 * input)
input = torch.tensor([[-1.0, 2.0], [0.0, -3.0]])
```

```
output = leaky_relu(input)
print(output)
```

Example Explanation:

- Implements a Leaky ReLU function that scales negative values by 0.01.
- Transforms the input tensor while avoiding zero gradients for negative inputs.

Real-Life Project

Project Name: Activation Function Exploration
Project Goal: Experiment with different activation functions and observe their impact on training a simple neural network.
Code for This Project:

```
import torch
import torch.nn as nn
import torch.optim as optim
from torchvision import datasets, transforms
from torch.utils.data import DataLoader

# Data preprocessing
transform = transforms.ToTensor()
train_dataset = datasets.MNIST(root='data', train=True,
transform=transform, download=True)
train_loader = DataLoader(train_dataset, batch_size=64,
shuffle=True)

# Define the model
class SimpleModel(nn.Module):
    def __init__(self):
        super(SimpleModel, self).__init__()
        self.fc1 = nn.Linear(28*28, 128)
        self.relu = nn.ReLU()
        self.fc2 = nn.Linear(128, 10)

    def forward(self, x):
        x = x.view(x.size(0), -1)
```

```python
        x = self.relu(self.fc1(x))
        return self.fc2(x)

model = SimpleModel()

# Define loss function and optimizer
criterion = nn.CrossEntropyLoss()
optimizer = optim.SGD(model.parameters(), lr=0.01)

# Training loop
epochs = 5
for epoch in range(epochs):
    for images, labels in train_loader:
        optimizer.zero_grad()
        outputs = model(images)
        loss = criterion(outputs, labels)
        loss.backward()
        optimizer.step()
    print(f"Epoch {epoch+1}/{epochs}, Loss:
{loss.item():.4f}")
print("Training complete.")
```
Expected Output:

- Training loss decreases over epochs.
- Model demonstrates the effect of ReLU activation on training efficiency.

Chapter - 15 Configuring the Training Process in PyTorch

Configuring the training process in PyTorch involves setting up essential components like data loaders, models, loss functions, optimizers, and training loops. A well-configured training pipeline ensures efficient and accurate model training. This chapter provides a detailed guide to configuring each element for successful neural network training in PyTorch.

Key Characteristics of Training Configuration

- **Data Preparation:** Use `DataLoader` for efficient data management.
- **Model Initialization:** Define the architecture with `torch.nn.Module`.
- **Loss Function:** Choose an appropriate loss to quantify prediction errors.
- **Optimizer:** Select an optimization algorithm to update weights.
- **Training Loop:** Execute forward and backward passes iteratively to optimize the model.
- **Device Management:** Leverage GPUs for accelerated training.

Steps to Configure Training in PyTorch

1. **Prepare the Dataset:** Load and preprocess data using `torch.utils.data.DataLoader`.
2. **Define the Model:** Create the model architecture using `torch.nn.Module`.
3. **Select Loss Function:** Pick a loss function suitable for the task.
4. **Initialize Optimizer:** Set up an optimizer with the model's parameters.
5. **Write the Training Loop:** Implement the forward and backward passes.
6. **Use GPUs:** Transfer data and model to the GPU for faster computation.

Syntax Table

SL No	Function	Syntax/Example	Description
1	Data Loading	`DataLoader(dataset, batch_size, shuffle=True)`	Loads data in batches for training.
2	Define Model	`class Model(nn.Module):`	Creates the model architecture.
3	Specify Loss Function	`criterion = nn.CrossEntropyLoss()`	Defines the loss function for classification tasks.
4	Set Optimizer	`optimizer = optim.SGD(model.parameters(), lr=0.01)`	Configures the optimization algorithm.
5	Training Loop	`for epoch in range(epochs):`	Iteratively trains the model over multiple epochs.
6	Use GPU	`model.to(device)`	Moves the model to the GPU for training.

Syntax Explanation

1. Data Loading
What is Data Loading?
Data loading involves preparing and feeding data to the model in mini-batches during training. PyTorch's `DataLoader` simplifies this process by handling batching, shuffling, and parallel data loading.
Syntax:
```
data_loader = DataLoader(dataset, batch_size=64, shuffle=True)
```
Detailed Explanation:
- **Purpose:** Efficiently manages data during training.
- **Parameters:**
    - `dataset`: The dataset to load.
    - `batch_size`: Number of samples per batch.

○   shuffle: Whether to shuffle data at each epoch.
- **Output:** An iterator that yields batches of data.

Example:

```
from torchvision import datasets, transforms
from torch.utils.data import DataLoader
transform = transforms.ToTensor()
dataset = datasets.MNIST(root='data', train=True,
transform=transform, download=True)
data_loader = DataLoader(dataset, batch_size=64,
shuffle=True)
```

Example Explanation:

- Loads the MNIST dataset with a batch size of 64.
- Applies transformations (e.g., converting images to tensors).
- Enables shuffling for randomized training.

2. Define Model

What is Model Definition?

Model definition involves creating the architecture of the neural network, specifying its layers and forward pass logic.

Syntax:

```
class Model(nn.Module):
    def __init__(self):
        super(Model, self).__init__()
        self.fc = nn.Linear(28*28, 10)
    def forward(self, x):
        return self.fc(x)
```

Detailed Explanation:

- **Purpose:** Encapsulates the neural network structure.
- **Components:**
    ○   __init__: Defines the layers of the model.
    ○   forward: Implements the forward pass logic.
- **Output:** A PyTorch model ready for training and inference.

Example:

```
model = Model()
print(model)
```

Example Explanation:
- Defines a simple model with one fully connected layer.
- Outputs the model's architecture.

3. Specify Loss Function
What is a Loss Function?
A loss function measures the discrepancy between the model's predictions and the true labels, guiding the optimization process.
Syntax:
```
criterion = nn.CrossEntropyLoss()
```
Detailed Explanation:
- **Purpose:** Quantifies prediction error.
- **Behavior:**
  - For classification, compares predicted probabilities to true labels.
  - Supports various loss types, e.g., MSE, CrossEntropy.
- **Output:** A scalar loss value.

Example:
```
outputs = torch.randn(64, 10)   # Batch of predictions
labels = torch.randint(0, 10, (64,))   # Ground truth
labels
loss = criterion(outputs, labels)
print(loss.item())
```
Example Explanation:
- Computes cross-entropy loss for a batch of predictions and labels.
- Outputs the loss as a scalar value.

4. Set Optimizer
What is an Optimizer?
An optimizer updates the model's parameters based on gradients computed during backpropagation.
Syntax:
```
optimizer = optim.SGD(model.parameters(), lr=0.01)
```
Detailed Explanation:
- **Purpose:** Adjusts weights to minimize the loss.
- **Parameters:**

- o `model.parameters()`: Trainable parameters of the model.
- o `lr`: Learning rate controlling step size.
- **Behavior:**
  - o Updates parameters using gradients.
  - o Supports different algorithms like SGD, Adam, etc.
- **Output:** An optimizer object for training.

Example:
```
optimizer = optim.Adam(model.parameters(), lr=0.001)
```
Example Explanation:
- Configures the Adam optimizer for adaptive learning.
- Prepares the optimizer for weight updates.

5. Training Loop
What is a Training Loop?
The training loop executes forward and backward passes iteratively, updating model weights to minimize the loss.
Syntax:
```
for epoch in range(epochs):
    for inputs, labels in data_loader:
        optimizer.zero_grad()
        outputs = model(inputs)
        loss = criterion(outputs, labels)
        loss.backward()
        optimizer.step()
```
Detailed Explanation:
- **Purpose:** Optimizes the model over multiple epochs.
- **Steps:**
  - o Zero gradients.
  - o Perform forward pass.
  - o Compute loss.
  - o Backpropagate gradients.
  - o Update parameters.
- **Output:** Trained model parameters.

Example:

```
for epoch in range(5):
    for images, labels in data_loader:
        images = images.view(images.size(0), -1)
        optimizer.zero_grad()
        outputs = model(images)
        loss = criterion(outputs, labels)
        loss.backward()
        optimizer.step()
    print(f"Epoch {epoch+1}, Loss: {loss.item():.4f}")
```

Example Explanation:

- Trains the model over 5 epochs.
- Prints the loss after each epoch.

6. Use GPU

What is GPU Utilization?

GPU utilization accelerates training by leveraging parallel computation.

Syntax:

```
device = torch.device("cuda" if
torch.cuda.is_available() else "cpu")
model = model.to(device)
```

Detailed Explanation:

- **Purpose:** Speeds up computation by transferring data and models to the GPU.
- **Behavior:**
  - Checks for GPU availability.
  - Moves tensors and models to the GPU.
- **Output:** Accelerated training performance.

Example:

```
inputs, labels = inputs.to(device), labels.to(device)
outputs = model(inputs)
```

Example Explanation:

- Moves input and label tensors to the GPU.
- Processes data on the GPU for faster computation.

Real-Life Project

Project Name: Configuring Training for MNIST Classification

Project Goal: Train a neural network to classify handwritten digits from the MNIST dataset.

Code for This Project:

```python
import torch
import torch.nn as nn
import torch.optim as optim
from torchvision import datasets, transforms
from torch.utils.data import DataLoader

# Data preprocessing
transform = transforms.ToTensor()
dataset = datasets.MNIST(root='data', train=True,
transform=transform, download=True)
data_loader = DataLoader(dataset, batch_size=64,
shuffle=True)

# Define the model
class MNISTModel(nn.Module):
    def __init__(self):
        super(MNISTModel, self).__init__()
        self.fc1 = nn.Linear(28*28, 128)
        self.fc2 = nn.Linear(128, 64)
        self.fc3 = nn.Linear(64, 10)

    def forward(self, x):
        x = x.view(x.size(0), -1)
        x = torch.relu(self.fc1(x))
        x = torch.relu(self.fc2(x))
        return self.fc3(x)
model = MNISTModel()

# Define loss function and optimizer
criterion = nn.CrossEntropyLoss()
optimizer = optim.SGD(model.parameters(), lr=0.01)
```

```python
# Training loop
epochs = 5
for epoch in range(epochs):
    for images, labels in data_loader:
        images = images.view(images.size(0), -1)
        optimizer.zero_grad()
        outputs = model(images)
        loss = criterion(outputs, labels)
        loss.backward()
        optimizer.step()
    print(f"Epoch {epoch+1}/{epochs}, Loss:
{loss.item():.4f}")
print("Training complete.")
```

Expected Output:

- Training loss decreases over epochs.
- The model learns to classify MNIST digits effectively.

Chapter - 16 Working with Loss Functions in PyTorch

Loss functions are a fundamental part of training neural networks in PyTorch. They quantify the discrepancy between the model's predictions and the actual labels, guiding the optimization process. PyTorch offers a wide range of pre-defined loss functions in the torch.nn module, while also allowing the creation of custom loss functions. This chapter explores the purpose, types, and implementation of loss functions in PyTorch.

Key Characteristics of Loss Functions

- **Quantification:** Measure the error between predictions and true labels.
- **Differentiability:** Ensure compatibility with gradient-based optimization.
- **Task-Specificity:** Tailored to specific tasks like classification or regression.
- **Pre-Defined Options:** Includes commonly used losses such as CrossEntropy and MSE.
- **Customizability:** Supports defining user-specific loss functions for unique requirements.

Steps to Use Loss Functions in PyTorch

1. **Select a Loss Function:** Choose from pre-defined options or define a custom function.
2. **Compute Loss:** Pass the model's predictions and true labels to the loss function.
3. **Integrate with Training Loop:** Use the loss value to compute gradients and update parameters.

Syntax Table

SL No	Function	Syntax/Example	Description
1	Cross-Entropy Loss	`criterion = nn.CrossEntropyLoss()`	Loss for classification tasks.
2	Mean Squared	`criterion =`	Loss for regression

		Error Loss	nn.MSELoss()	tasks.
3	Binary Cross-Entropy Loss	criterion = nn.BCELoss()	Loss for binary classification tasks.
4	Custom Loss Function	def custom_loss(outp ut, target):	Defines a user-specific loss function.
5	Compute Loss	loss = criterion(output , target)	Calculates the loss value.

Syntax Explanation

1. Cross-Entropy Loss

What is Cross-Entropy Loss?

Cross-Entropy Loss is widely used for multi-class classification tasks. It compares the predicted probability distribution with the true class labels.

Syntax:

```
criterion = nn.CrossEntropyLoss()
```

Detailed Explanation:

- **Purpose:** Measures the error between predicted probabilities and true class indices.
- **Parameters:**
    o input: Logits (unscaled predictions) from the model.
    o target: Ground truth class indices.
- **Behavior:**
    o Converts logits to probabilities using Softmax.
    o Computes the negative log-likelihood of the true class.
- **Output:** A scalar loss value.

Example:

```
import torch.nn as nn
import torch
criterion = nn.CrossEntropyLoss()
output = torch.tensor([[2.5, 0.3, 0.2], [0.1, 1.0,
1.5]])  # Logits
target = torch.tensor([0, 2])  # Ground truth
loss = criterion(output, target)
print(loss.item())
```

Example Explanation:

- The output contains unscaled predictions for two samples across three classes.
- The target specifies the true class index for each sample.
- The loss function computes the error, returning a scalar value.

2. Mean Squared Error Loss

What is Mean Squared Error Loss?

Mean Squared Error (MSE) Loss is used for regression tasks. It calculates the average squared difference between predicted and true values.

Syntax:

```
criterion = nn.MSELoss()
```

Detailed Explanation:

- **Purpose:** Measures the mean squared difference between predictions and targets.
- **Parameters:**
  - input: Predicted values.
  - target: True values.
- **Behavior:**
  - Computes (predicted - target)^2 for each element.
  - Averages the result over all elements.
- **Output:** A scalar loss value.

Example:

```
criterion = nn.MSELoss()
predicted = torch.tensor([2.5, 0.0, 2.1])
true = torch.tensor([3.0, -0.5, 2.0])
loss = criterion(predicted, true)
print(loss.item())
```

Example Explanation:

- Calculates the squared differences: (2.5-3.0)^2, (0.0-(-0.5))^2, (2.1-2.0)^2.
- Computes the average of these values to return the loss.

3. Binary Cross-Entropy Loss

What is Binary Cross-Entropy Loss?

Binary Cross-Entropy Loss is used for binary classification tasks. It works on probabilities that represent binary outcomes.

Syntax:

```
criterion = nn.BCELoss()
```

Detailed Explanation:

- **Purpose:** Measures the error between predicted probabilities and binary targets.
- **Parameters:**
    - `input`: Predicted probabilities.
    - `target`: Binary ground truth values (0 or 1).
- **Behavior:**
    - Applies the formula: `-target*log(prediction) - (1-target)*log(1-prediction)`.
    - Computes the average loss over all elements.
- **Output:** A scalar loss value.

Example:

```
criterion = nn.BCELoss()
predicted = torch.tensor([0.8, 0.1, 0.9])
true = torch.tensor([1.0, 0.0, 1.0])
loss = criterion(predicted, true)
print(loss.item())
```

Example Explanation:

- Uses the predicted probabilities and binary targets.
- Computes the average binary cross-entropy loss for the inputs.

4. Custom Loss Function

What is a Custom Loss Function?

A custom loss function is defined by the user to meet specific requirements not covered by pre-defined options.

Syntax:

```
def custom_loss(output, target):
    return torch.mean((output - target)**2)
```

Detailed Explanation:

- **Purpose:** Allows flexibility in defining unique loss computations.
- **Parameters:**
  - output: Predicted values.
  - target: True values.
- **Behavior:**
  - Executes user-defined computations on the input tensors.
- **Output:** A scalar loss value.

Example:

```
def smooth_l1_loss(output, target):
    diff = torch.abs(output - target)
    loss = torch.where(diff < 1, 0.5 * diff**2, diff -
0.5)
    return torch.mean(loss)


predicted = torch.tensor([2.5, 0.0, 2.1])
true = torch.tensor([3.0, -0.5, 2.0])
loss = smooth_l1_loss(predicted, true)
print(loss.item())
```

Example Explanation:

- Implements a Smooth L1 Loss, blending L1 and L2 losses for robustness.
- Calculates and averages the element-wise loss values.

Real-Life Project

Project Name: Loss Function Comparison for MNIST

Project Goal: Train a neural network to classify MNIST digits using different loss functions and observe their impact.

Code for This Project:

```
import torch
import torch.nn as nn
import torch.optim as optim
from torchvision import datasets, transforms
from torch.utils.data import DataLoader
# Data preprocessing
transform = transforms.ToTensor()
dataset = datasets.MNIST(root='data', train=True,
```

```python
                       transform=transform, download=True)
data_loader = DataLoader(dataset, batch_size=64,
shuffle=True)
# Define the model
class MNISTModel(nn.Module):
    def __init__(self):
        super(MNISTModel, self).__init__()
        self.fc1 = nn.Linear(28*28, 128)
        self.fc2 = nn.Linear(128, 64)
        self.fc3 = nn.Linear(64, 10)
    def forward(self, x):
        x = x.view(x.size(0), -1)
        x = torch.relu(self.fc1(x))
        x = torch.relu(self.fc2(x))
        return self.fc3(x)
model = MNISTModel()
# Define loss function and optimizer
criterion = nn.CrossEntropyLoss()
optimizer = optim.SGD(model.parameters(), lr=0.01)
# Training loop
epochs = 5
for epoch in range(epochs):
    for images, labels in data_loader:
        images = images.view(images.size(0), -1)
        optimizer.zero_grad()
        outputs = model(images)
        loss = criterion(outputs, labels)
        loss.backward()
        optimizer.step()
    print(f"Epoch {epoch+1}/{epochs}, Loss:
{loss.item():.4f}")
print("Training complete.")
```

Expected Output:

- Training loss decreases over epochs.
- Observations highlight the behavior of the selected loss function.

Chapter - 17 Optimization Techniques with PyTorch Optimizers

Optimization techniques are the cornerstone of training neural networks, enabling models to minimize loss functions and improve performance. PyTorch provides a variety of optimization algorithms through its `torch.optim` module, each suited for specific types of models and tasks. This chapter explores common optimizers, their configurations, and how they integrate into a training pipeline.

Key Characteristics of PyTorch Optimizers

- **Gradient-Based:** Updates parameters using gradients computed during backpropagation.
- **Customizable:** Supports fine-tuning with learning rates and other hyperparameters.
- **Wide Range:** Includes popular optimizers like SGD, Adam, and RMSprop.
- **Efficient:** Designed for compatibility with PyTorch's dynamic computation graph.
- **Extensible:** Allows users to implement custom optimizers.

Steps to Use Optimizers in PyTorch

1. **Initialize Optimizer:** Define an optimizer with the model's parameters.
2. **Set Learning Rate:** Choose an appropriate learning rate for the task.
3. **Zero Gradients:** Clear gradients before backpropagation.
4. **Perform Parameter Update:** Apply the optimizer after computing gradients.
5. **Adjust Learning Rate:** Optionally modify the learning rate during training.

Syntax Table

SL No	Function	Syntax/Example	Description
1	Define SGD Optimizer	`optimizer = optim.SGD(model.par ameters(), lr=0.01)`	Stochastic Gradient Descent.
2	Define Adam Optimizer	`optimizer = optim.Adam(model.pa rameters(), lr=0.001)`	Adaptive Moment Estimation.
3	Zero Gradients	`optimizer.zero_grad ()`	Clears accumulated gradients.
4	Update Parameters	`optimizer.step()`	Updates model parameters based on gradients.
5	Learning Rate Scheduler	`scheduler = lr_scheduler.StepLR (optimizer, step_size=10, gamma=0.1)`	Adjusts learning rate during training.

Syntax Explanation

1. Define SGD Optimizer

What is SGD?

Stochastic Gradient Descent (SGD) is a widely used optimization algorithm that updates model parameters by moving them in the direction of the negative gradient.

Syntax:

`optimizer = optim.SGD(model.parameters(), lr=0.01)`

Detailed Explanation:

- **Purpose:** Minimizes the loss function by adjusting weights using gradients.
- **Parameters:**
    - `model.parameters()`: Trainable parameters of the model.
    - `lr`: Learning rate determining the step size for updates.

- **Behavior:**
  - o Computes parameter updates based on the gradient of the loss function.
  - o Optionally supports momentum for faster convergence.
- **Output:** An optimizer object ready for use in training.

Example:
```
optimizer = optim.SGD(model.parameters(), lr=0.01,
momentum=0.9)
```
Example Explanation:
- Configures SGD with momentum to accelerate convergence.
- Combines past gradients with the current one for smoother updates.

2. Define Adam Optimizer
What is Adam?
Adam (Adaptive Moment Estimation) is an adaptive learning rate optimization algorithm that adjusts learning rates based on moment estimates of gradients.

Syntax:
```
optimizer = optim.Adam(model.parameters(), lr=0.001)
```
Detailed Explanation:
- **Purpose:** Provides efficient and adaptive learning rate updates.
- **Parameters:**
  - o `model.parameters()`: Trainable parameters of the model.
  - o `lr`: Initial learning rate.
  - o Optional parameters like `betas` (default `(0.9, 0.999)`) control the exponential decay rates for moment estimates.
- **Behavior:**
  - o Maintains moving averages of gradients and squared gradients.
  - o Updates parameters using these averages to balance speed and stability.
- **Output:** An optimizer object with adaptive capabilities.

Example:

```
optimizer = optim.Adam(model.parameters(), lr=0.001,
weight_decay=1e-5)
```

Example Explanation:

- Configures Adam with weight decay to regularize the model and prevent overfitting.
- Adapts learning rates during training for optimal performance.

3. Zero Gradients

What is Zeroing Gradients?

Zeroing gradients ensures that gradients from the previous iteration do not accumulate during backpropagation.

Syntax:

```
optimizer.zero_grad()
```

Detailed Explanation:

- **Purpose:** Clears the gradient buffers before computing new gradients.
- **Behavior:**
  - Prevents gradients from accumulating across iterations.
  - Ensures the optimizer updates parameters based solely on the current batch.
- **Output:** Clears gradients; no tensor is returned.

Example:

```
optimizer.zero_grad()
```

Example Explanation:

- Prepares the model for a new round of gradient computation.
- Ensures accurate and independent updates for each training step.

4. Update Parameters

What is Updating Parameters?

Parameter updates adjust the model's weights based on the computed gradients and the optimizer's algorithm.

Syntax:

```
optimizer.step()
```

Detailed Explanation:
- **Purpose:** Applies the computed gradients to update model parameters.
- **Behavior:**
  - Uses the optimizer's algorithm (e.g., SGD, Adam) to modify weights.
  - Considers learning rates, momentum, and other hyperparameters.
- **Output:** Updates weights in place; no tensor is returned.

Example:
```
optimizer.step()
```
Example Explanation:
- Applies gradient-based updates to the model's parameters.
- Ensures that weights are optimized to minimize the loss function.

5. Learning Rate Scheduler
What is a Learning Rate Scheduler?
Learning rate schedulers dynamically adjust the learning rate during training to improve convergence.

Syntax:
```
scheduler = lr_scheduler.StepLR(optimizer,
step_size=10, gamma=0.1)
```
Detailed Explanation:
- **Purpose:** Reduces the learning rate at specified intervals to fine-tune updates as training progresses.
- **Parameters:**
  - `optimizer`: The optimizer whose learning rate will be adjusted.
  - `step_size`: The number of epochs between adjustments.
  - `gamma`: The factor by which the learning rate is multiplied.
- **Behavior:**
  - Decays the learning rate to encourage stable convergence.
  - Supports various scheduling strategies like `StepLR`, `ExponentialLR`, etc.
- **Output:** A scheduler object linked to the optimizer.

Example:

```
scheduler = lr_scheduler.StepLR(optimizer,
step_size=10, gamma=0.1)
for epoch in range(30):
    train_one_epoch()
    scheduler.step()
```

Example Explanation:

- Reduces the learning rate every 10 epochs by a factor of 0.1.
- Enhances stability as the model approaches optimal performance.

Real-Life Project

Project Name: Optimizing Training with Adam and Learning Rate Scheduling

Project Goal: Train a neural network on the CIFAR-10 dataset using Adam optimizer and a learning rate scheduler.

Code for This Project:

```
import torch
import torch.nn as nn
import torch.optim as optim
from torchvision import datasets, transforms
from torch.optim import lr_scheduler
from torch.utils.data import DataLoader

# Data preprocessing
transform = transforms.Compose([
    transforms.ToTensor(),
    transforms.Normalize((0.5,), (0.5,))
])
train_dataset = datasets.CIFAR10(root='data',
train=True, transform=transform, download=True)
train_loader = DataLoader(train_dataset, batch_size=64,
shuffle=True)

# Define the model
class SimpleCNN(nn.Module):
    def __init__(self):
```

```python
        super(SimpleCNN, self).__init__()
        self.conv1 = nn.Conv2d(3, 16, kernel_size=3,
stride=1, padding=1)
        self.pool = nn.MaxPool2d(kernel_size=2,
stride=2, padding=0)
        self.fc = nn.Linear(16 * 16 * 16, 10)

    def forward(self, x):
        x = self.pool(torch.relu(self.conv1(x)))
        x = x.view(x.size(0), -1)
        x = self.fc(x)
        return x


model = SimpleCNN()
# Define optimizer and scheduler
criterion = nn.CrossEntropyLoss()
optimizer = optim.Adam(model.parameters(), lr=0.001)
scheduler = lr_scheduler.StepLR(optimizer,
step_size=10, gamma=0.1)
# Training loop
epochs = 20
for epoch in range(epochs):
    for images, labels in train_loader:
        optimizer.zero_grad()
        outputs = model(images)
        loss = criterion(outputs, labels)
        loss.backward()
        optimizer.step()
    scheduler.step()
    print(f"Epoch {epoch+1}/{epochs}, Loss:
{loss.item():.4f}")
print("Training complete.")
```

Expected Output:

- Training loss decreases over epochs.
- Learning rate reduces periodically, stabilizing training performance.

Chapter -18 Monitoring Training with TensorBoard and Other Tools

Monitoring the training process is crucial for understanding a model's performance, identifying issues, and improving efficiency. PyTorch provides seamless integration with TensorBoard, a visualization tool that tracks metrics, visualizes model architectures, and logs other key information. Additionally, various third-party tools and PyTorch's inbuilt utilities help monitor training in real time. This chapter explores using TensorBoard and other tools for effective training monitoring.

Key Characteristics of Training Monitoring

- **Metric Visualization:** Plots loss, accuracy, and other metrics over epochs.
- **Model Inspection:** Displays model architecture and parameter distributions.
- **Real-Time Feedback:** Tracks progress during training.
- **Customization:** Logs custom metrics and additional information.
- **Compatibility:** Integrates with PyTorch and third-party tools.

Steps to Use TensorBoard in PyTorch

1. **Install TensorBoard:** Ensure TensorBoard is installed (`pip install tensorboard`).
2. **Initialize SummaryWriter:** Create a writer to log metrics and other data.
3. **Log Metrics:** Record training loss, accuracy, and other values.
4. **Launch TensorBoard:** Start TensorBoard to view the logged information.
5. **Integrate with Model:** Log model graphs, parameter distributions, and more.

Syntax Table

SL No	Function	Syntax/Example	Description
1	Initialize SummaryWriter	`writer = SummaryWriter(log_dir="logs")`	Creates a writer to log data for TensorBoard.
2	Log Scalar Values	`writer.add_scalar(tag, scalar_value, step)`	Records a scalar value (e.g., loss, accuracy).
3	Log Model Graph	`writer.add_graph(model, input_to_model)`	Visualizes the model architecture.
4	Log Parameter Histograms	`writer.add_histogram(tag, values, step)`	Logs parameter distributions over training.
5	Launch TensorBoard	`tensorboard --logdir=logs`	Starts the TensorBoard server to view logs.

Syntax Explanation

1. Initialize SummaryWriter
What is SummaryWriter?
The SummaryWriter class initializes a logger that writes data for TensorBoard visualization.
Syntax:
```
from torch.utils.tensorboard import SummaryWriter
writer = SummaryWriter(log_dir="logs")
```
Detailed Explanation:
- **Purpose:** Creates a directory to store logs for TensorBoard.
- **Parameters:**
    - `log_dir`: Path to the directory where logs will be saved.
    - Optional parameters allow customization like flushing frequency.
- **Output:** A SummaryWriter object used for logging data.

Example:

```
writer = SummaryWriter(log_dir="logs/training")
```

Example Explanation:
- Initializes a writer that saves logs in the `logs/training` directory.
- Enables subsequent logging of metrics and other information.

2. Log Scalar Values

What are Scalar Values?

Scalar values are single numerical metrics, such as loss or accuracy, tracked during training.

Syntax:

```
writer.add_scalar(tag, scalar_value, step)
```

Detailed Explanation:
- **Purpose:** Tracks changes in scalar metrics over time.
- **Parameters:**
    - `tag`: Label for the metric (e.g., "loss").
    - `scalar_value`: The value to log.
    - `step`: The training step or epoch associated with the value.
- **Output:** Writes the scalar value to the log for TensorBoard visualization.

Example:

```
for epoch in range(10):
    loss = compute_loss()  # Hypothetical loss function
    writer.add_scalar("Training Loss", loss, epoch)
```

Example Explanation:
- Logs the training loss for each epoch.
- Visualized as a line plot in TensorBoard.

3. Log Model Graph

What is Model Graph Logging?

Model graph logging visualizes the structure of a neural network, including layers and data flow.

Syntax:

```
writer.add_graph(model, input_to_model)
```

Detailed Explanation:

- **Purpose:** Displays the model's computational graph in TensorBoard.
- **Parameters:**
  - `model`: The PyTorch model to log.
  - `input_to_model`: A sample input tensor to pass through the model.
- **Behavior:**
  - Generates the graph by tracing the model's forward pass.
- **Output:** A graph visualization in TensorBoard.

Example:
```
model = MyModel()
sample_input = torch.randn(1, 3, 32, 32)  # Example
input for a CNN
writer.add_graph(model, sample_input)
```

Example Explanation:

- Logs the graph of a convolutional neural network (CNN).
- Visualizes data flow from input to output through the network.

4. Log Parameter Histograms

What are Parameter Histograms?

Histograms visualize the distribution of model parameters, such as weights and biases, over training.

Syntax:
```
writer.add_histogram(tag, values, step)
```

Detailed Explanation:

- **Purpose:** Tracks changes in parameter distributions over time.
- **Parameters:**
  - `tag`: Label for the histogram (e.g., "weights_layer1").
  - `values`: Tensor containing parameter values.
  - `step`: Training step or epoch associated with the values.
- **Output:** A histogram visualization in TensorBoard.

Example:
```
for name, param in model.named_parameters():
    writer.add_histogram(name, param, epoch)
```

Example Explanation:
- Logs histograms for all model parameters at each epoch.
- Visualizes how weights and biases change during training.

5. Launch TensorBoard

What is Launching TensorBoard?

Launching TensorBoard opens a web interface to view logged data, including metrics, graphs, and distributions.

Syntax:

```
tensorboard --logdir=logs
```

Detailed Explanation:
- **Purpose:** Provides a user-friendly interface to explore logged data.
- **Parameters:**
    - `--logdir`: Path to the directory containing TensorBoard logs.
- **Behavior:**
    - Starts a local web server for visualization.
    - Accessible at `http://localhost:6006` by default.

Example:

```
tensorboard --logdir=logs/training
```

Example Explanation:
- Opens TensorBoard for logs stored in the `logs/training` directory.
- Displays metrics, graphs, and histograms.

Real-Life Project

Project Name: Monitoring Training Metrics for CIFAR-10
Project Goal: Train a CNN on CIFAR-10 while logging metrics and visualizations using TensorBoard.
Code for This Project:

```
import torch
import torch.nn as nn
import torch.optim as optim
from torchvision import datasets, transforms
from torch.utils.tensorboard import SummaryWriter
from torch.utils.data import DataLoader
```

```python
# Data preprocessing
transform = transforms.Compose([
    transforms.ToTensor(),
    transforms.Normalize((0.5,), (0.5,))
])
train_dataset = datasets.CIFAR10(root='data',
train=True, transform=transform, download=True)
train_loader = DataLoader(train_dataset, batch_size=64,
shuffle=True)

# Define the model
class SimpleCNN(nn.Module):
    def __init__(self):
        super(SimpleCNN, self).__init__()
        self.conv1 = nn.Conv2d(3, 16, kernel_size=3,
stride=1, padding=1)
        self.pool = nn.MaxPool2d(kernel_size=2,
stride=2, padding=0)
        self.fc = nn.Linear(16 * 16 * 16, 10)

    def forward(self, x):
        x = self.pool(torch.relu(self.conv1(x)))
        x = x.view(x.size(0), -1)
        x = self.fc(x)
        return x

model = SimpleCNN()

# Define optimizer and criterion
criterion = nn.CrossEntropyLoss()
optimizer = optim.Adam(model.parameters(), lr=0.001)

# Initialize TensorBoard writer
writer = SummaryWriter(log_dir="logs/cifar10")

# Training loop
```

```
epochs = 10
for epoch in range(epochs):
    for images, labels in train_loader:
        optimizer.zero_grad()
        outputs = model(images)
        loss = criterion(outputs, labels)
        loss.backward()
        optimizer.step()
    writer.add_scalar("Training Loss", loss.item(),
epoch)

# Log model graph
sample_input = torch.randn(1, 3, 32, 32)
writer.add_graph(model, sample_input)

print("Training complete. Run 'tensorboard --
logdir=logs/cifar10' to view logs.")
```
Expected Output:
- Metrics like loss are visualized in TensorBoard.
- Model graph and parameter histograms provide additional insights.

Chapter - 19 Implementing Early Stopping and Checkpoints in PyTorch

Early stopping and model checkpoints are essential techniques for training neural networks efficiently. Early stopping prevents overfitting by halting training when performance on validation data stops improving, while checkpoints save model states during training, allowing recovery or future reuse. This chapter explains how to implement these techniques in PyTorch, ensuring better training control and resource utilization.

Key Characteristics of Early Stopping and Checkpoints

- **Overfitting Prevention:** Stops training once validation performance stagnates.
- **Recovery:** Allows resuming training from saved checkpoints.
- **Efficiency:** Saves time and computational resources by avoiding unnecessary epochs.
- **Flexibility:** Configurable conditions for stopping and saving models.
- **Integration:** Seamlessly integrates into PyTorch training loops.

Steps to Implement Early Stopping and Checkpoints

1. **Track Validation Performance:** Monitor metrics like loss or accuracy on validation data.
2. **Define Stopping Criteria:** Specify conditions for stopping training.
3. **Save Checkpoints:** Store model and optimizer states periodically or based on performance.
4. **Resume Training:** Load checkpoints to continue training if needed.

Syntax Table

SL No	Function	Syntax/Example	Description
1	Save Checkpoint	`torch.save(state, PATH)`	Saves model and optimizer states.
2	Load Checkpoint	`state = torch.load(PATH)`	Loads model and optimizer states.
3	Define Early Stopping	Custom logic based on validation performance.	Implements criteria to stop training.
4	Monitor Metrics	Compute metrics on validation data.	Tracks validation loss, accuracy, or other values.
5	Resume Training	Restore model and optimizer from a checkpoint.	Allows continuing training from a saved state.

Syntax Explanation

1. Save Checkpoint
What is a Checkpoint?
A checkpoint stores the model's parameters, optimizer state, and additional information to allow resuming or analyzing training later.
Syntax:
`torch.save(state, PATH)`
Detailed Explanation:
- **Purpose:** Saves the model and optimizer states to a file.
- **Parameters:**
  - `state`: A dictionary containing model state, optimizer state, epoch, and other data.
  - PATH: File path to save the checkpoint.
- **Behavior:** Writes the dictionary to disk for later retrieval.
- **Output:** Saves the checkpoint file.

Example:
```
state = {
    'epoch': epoch,
    'model_state': model.state_dict(),
    'optimizer_state': optimizer.state_dict(),
    'loss': loss
}
torch.save(state, 'checkpoint.pth')
```
Example Explanation:
- Saves the current training epoch, model state, optimizer state, and loss to a file.
- Enables resuming training from this point.

2. Load Checkpoint
What is Loading a Checkpoint?
Loading a checkpoint restores the model and optimizer to their saved states.
Syntax:
```
state = torch.load(PATH)
```
Detailed Explanation:
- **Purpose:** Retrieves the saved state from a checkpoint file.
- **Parameters:**
    o   PATH: File path to the saved checkpoint.

- **Behavior:**
    o   Reads the file and loads the dictionary into memory.
    o   Allows restoring the model and optimizer states.
- **Output:** A dictionary containing the saved state.

Example:
```
state = torch.load('checkpoint.pth')
model.load_state_dict(state['model_state'])
optimizer.load_state_dict(state['optimizer_state'])
epoch = state['epoch']
```
Example Explanation:
- Restores the model, optimizer, and training epoch from the checkpoint.

- Resumes training from where it left off.

3. Define Early Stopping
What is Early Stopping?
Early stopping halts training when validation performance stops improving, preventing overfitting and saving resources.
Syntax:
```
if validation_loss > best_loss:
    trigger += 1
    if trigger >= patience:
        stop_training = True
```
Detailed Explanation:
- **Purpose:** Monitors validation performance and stops training if no improvement is observed for a specified number of epochs.
- **Parameters:**
    - `validation_loss`: Current validation loss.
    - `best_loss`: Best validation loss observed so far.
    - `patience`: Number of epochs to wait before stopping.
- **Behavior:**
    - Compares current loss with the best loss.
    - Increments a counter if no improvement is observed.
    - Stops training if the counter exceeds patience.
- **Output:** Updates a stopping condition.
Example:
```
patience = 5
trigger = 0
best_loss = float('inf')
for epoch in range(epochs):
    validation_loss = compute_validation_loss()
    if validation_loss < best_loss:
        best_loss = validation_loss
        trigger = 0
    else:
        trigger += 1
        if trigger >= patience:
            print("Early stopping triggered.")
            break
```

Example Explanation:

- Stops training if validation loss does not improve for 5 consecutive epochs.
- Ensures resources are not wasted on unnecessary training.

4. Monitor Metrics
What is Metric Monitoring?
Metric monitoring tracks validation loss, accuracy, or other metrics during training.

Syntax:
```
validation_loss = criterion(model(validation_data),
validation_labels)
```
Detailed Explanation:

- **Purpose:** Provides real-time feedback on model performance.
- **Behavior:**
  - Computes metrics using the validation dataset.
  - Logs metrics for visualization or stopping criteria.
- **Output:** A scalar value representing the metric.

Example:
```
validation_loss = criterion(model(validation_data),
validation_labels)
print(f"Validation Loss: {validation_loss.item()}")
```
Example Explanation:

- Calculates validation loss at each epoch.
- Prints the loss for real-time monitoring.

5. Resume Training
What is Resuming Training?
Resuming training involves restoring the model, optimizer, and other states from a checkpoint to continue training.

Syntax:
```
state = torch.load(PATH)
model.load_state_dict(state['model_state'])
optimizer.load_state_dict(state['optimizer_state'])
```
Detailed Explanation:

- **Purpose:** Allows training to continue from a saved state.

- **Parameters:**
  - ○ PATH: File path to the checkpoint.
  - ○ state: Dictionary containing saved states.
- **Behavior:**
  - ○ Restores model and optimizer states.
  - ○ Resumes training without restarting.
- **Output:** Resumes training seamlessly.

Example:

```
state = torch.load('checkpoint.pth')
model.load_state_dict(state['model_state'])
optimizer.load_state_dict(state['optimizer_state'])
epoch = state['epoch'] + 1
for epoch in range(epoch, epochs):
    train_one_epoch()
```

Example Explanation:

- Loads a saved checkpoint and continues training from the next epoch.
- Avoids losing progress due to interruptions.

Real-Life Project

Project Name: Early Stopping and Checkpointing for MNIST Classification
Project Goal: Train a neural network on the MNIST dataset with early stopping and checkpointing to save the best model.
Code for This Project:

```
import torch
import torch.nn as nn
import torch.optim as optim
from torchvision import datasets, transforms
from torch.utils.data import DataLoader

# Data preprocessing
transform = transforms.ToTensor()
dataset = datasets.MNIST(root='data', train=True,
transform=transform, download=True)
data_loader = DataLoader(dataset, batch_size=64,
shuffle=True)
```

```python
# Define the model
class SimpleNN(nn.Module):
    def __init__(self):
        super(SimpleNN, self).__init__()
        self.fc1 = nn.Linear(28*28, 128)
        self.fc2 = nn.Linear(128, 64)
        self.fc3 = nn.Linear(64, 10)

    def forward(self, x):
        x = x.view(x.size(0), -1)
        x = torch.relu(self.fc1(x))
        x = torch.relu(self.fc2(x))
        return self.fc3(x)


model = SimpleNN()
# Define loss function and optimizer
criterion = nn.CrossEntropyLoss()
optimizer = optim.SGD(model.parameters(), lr=0.01)

# Early stopping and checkpointing
best_loss = float('inf')
patience = 5
trigger = 0
for epoch in range(20):
    for images, labels in data_loader:
        optimizer.zero_grad()
        outputs = model(images)
        loss = criterion(outputs, labels)
        loss.backward()
        optimizer.step()

    validation_loss = loss.item()  # Example validation
loss
    if validation_loss < best_loss:
        best_loss = validation_loss
        trigger = 0
```

```
        torch.save({'model_state': model.state_dict(),
'optimizer_state': optimizer.state_dict(), 'epoch':
epoch}, 'best_model.pth')
    else:
        trigger += 1
        if trigger >= patience:
            print("Early stopping triggered.")
            break
print("Training complete.")
```

Expected Output:

- Training stops if validation loss does not improve for 5 epochs.
- The best model is saved as `best_model.pth` for later use.

Chapter - 20 Customizing Autograd for Complex Models

Autograd is PyTorch's automatic differentiation engine, enabling efficient computation of gradients for optimizing models. While PyTorch's built-in functionality suffices for most cases, complex models or custom operations may require manual gradient computation. This chapter explores how to customize autograd by defining new operations, overriding gradients, and creating custom `Function` classes.

Key Characteristics of Customizing Autograd:
- **Automatic Differentiation:** Automatically computes gradients for tensor operations.
- **Custom Gradients:** Allows manual definition of backward passes for specialized operations.
- **Integration:** Seamlessly integrates custom operations with PyTorch's optimization framework.
- **Efficiency:** Optimized for memory usage and computational performance.

Steps to Customize Autograd:
1. **Understand Default Behavior:** Learn how PyTorch's autograd computes gradients by default.
2. **Create Custom Functions:** Define new operations by subclassing `torch.autograd.Function`.
3. **Define Forward Pass:** Implement the computation logic in the `forward` method.
4. **Define Backward Pass:** Specify how gradients are calculated in the `backward` method.
5. **Use Custom Functions in Models:** Integrate these functions into PyTorch models seamlessly.

Syntax Table:

SL No	Function	Syntax/Example	Description
1	Subclass Function	`class CustomOp(Functi on)`	Creates a custom autograd function.
2	Define Forward Pass	`def forward(ctx, inputs):`	Implements the computation logic.
3	Define Backward Pass	`def backward(ctx, grad_output):`	Computes gradients for the custom operation.
4	Use Custom Function	`result = CustomOp.apply( inputs)`	Applies the custom operation in models.
5	Check Gradient Flow	`inputs.requires _grad_()`	Ensures gradients are tracked for tensors.

Syntax Explanation:

1. Subclass Function
What is Subclassing Function?
Subclassing `Function` involves creating custom autograd operations by defining their forward and backward passes. This is useful when standard PyTorch operations cannot express your computation.
Syntax:
```
from torch.autograd import Function
class CustomOp(Function):
    @staticmethod
    def forward(ctx, inputs):
        pass
    @staticmethod
    def backward(ctx, grad_output):
        pass
```

Detailed Explanation:

- **Purpose:** Enables definition of new operations with custom gradient computation.
- **Components:**
  - forward: Executes the operation and saves context for backpropagation.
  - backward: Computes gradients for the operation during backpropagation.
- **Output:** A reusable class that can be applied to tensors.

Example:
```
class Square(Function):
    @staticmethod
    def forward(ctx, inputs):
        ctx.save_for_backward(inputs)
        return inputs ** 2
    @staticmethod
    def backward(ctx, grad_output):
        inputs, = ctx.saved_tensors
        return 2 * inputs * grad_output
```
Example Explanation:

- Defines a Square operation that computes the square of inputs.
- Saves inputs for reuse in the backward pass.
- Computes the gradient $\partial 2 \cdot x \cdot \partial L / \partial y$ during backpropagation.

2. Define Forward Pass
What is the Forward Pass?
The forward pass specifies how input tensors are transformed into output tensors during the computation phase.

Syntax:
```
@staticmethod
def forward(ctx, inputs):
    pass
```
Detailed Explanation:

- **Purpose:** Implements the actual computation performed by the custom operation.
- **Parameters:**

- o ctx: Context object to store information for the backward pass.
  - o inputs: Input tensors for the operation.
- **Behavior:**
  - o Performs tensor computations.
  - o Stores data in ctx for use in the backward pass.
- **Output:** Returns transformed tensors as outputs.

Example:

```
@staticmethod
def forward(ctx, inputs):
    ctx.save_for_backward(inputs)
    return inputs ** 2
```

Example Explanation:
- Computes the square of the inputs.
- Saves inputs for later use in the backward pass.

3. Define Backward Pass

What is the Backward Pass?

The backward pass defines how gradients of the outputs are used to compute gradients of the inputs.

Syntax:

```
@staticmethod
def backward(ctx, grad_output):
    pass
```

Detailed Explanation:
- **Purpose:** Implements gradient computation for the custom operation.
- **Parameters:**
  - o ctx: Context object storing information from the forward pass.
  - o grad_output: Gradients of the outputs provided by downstream layers.
- **Behavior:**
  - o Retrieves saved tensors from ctx.
  - o Computes gradients with respect to the inputs.
- **Output:** Returns gradients for each input tensor.

Example:
```
@staticmethod
def backward(ctx, grad_output):
    inputs, = ctx.saved_tensors
    return 2 * inputs * grad_output
```
Example Explanation:
- Retrieves saved inputs from the context.
- Computes the gradient of the square operation as 2 * inputs * grad_output.

4. Use Custom Function

What is Using a Custom Function?

Using a custom function involves applying the defined forward and backward operations to tensors in a model or computation.

Syntax:
```
result = CustomOp.apply(inputs)
```
Detailed Explanation:
- **Purpose:** Executes the custom operation and integrates it into the computation graph.
- **Parameters:**
  - inputs: Input tensors for the operation.
- **Behavior:**
  - Executes the forward method.
  - Tracks the operation for gradient computation during backpropagation.
- **Output:** Transformed tensor(s) resulting from the custom operation.

Example:
```
inputs = torch.tensor([2.0, 3.0], requires_grad=True)
outputs = Square.apply(inputs)
outputs.backward(torch.tensor([1.0, 1.0]))
print(inputs.grad)
```
Example Explanation:
- Applies the custom Square function to inputs.
- Computes gradients using the defined backward pass.
- Outputs gradients $\partial 2 \cdot inputs$.

5. Check Gradient Flow

What is Checking Gradient Flow?

Checking gradient flow ensures that tensors are configured to track and compute gradients during backpropagation.

Syntax:

```
inputs.requires_grad_()
```

Detailed Explanation:

- **Purpose:** Enables gradient tracking for a tensor.
- **Parameters:**
  - None, but modifies the tensor in place.
- **Behavior:**
  - Sets the `requires_grad` attribute to True.
  - Tracks operations for automatic differentiation.
- **Output:** The modified tensor with `requires_grad=True`.

Example:

```
inputs = torch.tensor([1.0, 2.0, 3.0])
inputs.requires_grad_()
print(inputs.requires_grad)
```

Example Explanation:

- Enables gradient tracking for the `inputs` tensor.
- Outputs: True, indicating gradients will be computed.

Real-Life Project:

Project Name: Custom Gradient Clipping Operation
Project Goal: Implement a custom autograd function to clip gradients during backpropagation, preventing exploding gradients in deep networks.
Code for This Project:

```
import torch
from torch.autograd import Function
class GradientClip(Function):
    @staticmethod
    def forward(ctx, inputs, clip_value):
        ctx.save_for_backward(inputs)
        ctx.clip_value = clip_value
        return inputs
```

```python
    @staticmethod
    def backward(ctx, grad_output):
        inputs, = ctx.saved_tensors
        clip_value = ctx.clip_value
        grad_output = torch.clamp(grad_output, -
clip_value, clip_value)
        return grad_output, None
# Usage
inputs = torch.tensor([1.0, -2.0, 3.0],
requires_grad=True)
outputs = GradientClip.apply(inputs, 1.0)
outputs.backward(torch.tensor([1.0, 1.0, 1.0]))
print(inputs.grad)
```

Expected Output:

- Gradients are clipped to the range [-1.0, 1.0].
- Outputs: `tensor([ 1.0, -1.0, 1.0])`.

Chapter - 21 Working with PyTorch's Functional API

PyTorch's Functional API provides a versatile way to perform operations on tensors and build models. Unlike `torch.nn.Module`, which abstracts layers, the Functional API offers granular control over computations, enabling users to directly apply operations without creating full layers. This chapter covers how to leverage PyTorch's Functional API to implement custom operations and models.

Key Characteristics of the Functional API:
- **Granular Control:** Allows precise implementation of computations.
- **Stateless Operations:** Functional layers do not manage weights or biases.
- **Flexibility:** Facilitates dynamic behavior within models.
- **Interoperability:** Can be combined with `torch.nn.Module` for hybrid designs.
- **Extensibility:** Ideal for creating custom layer-like structures.

Steps to Use the Functional API:
1. **Import Functional API:** Access operations from `torch.nn.functional`.
2. **Perform Stateless Operations:** Use functions like `F.relu` or `F.linear` for computations.
3. **Design Custom Layers:** Combine Functional API calls in custom layers.
4. **Integrate with Modules:** Use Functional API within `torch.nn.Module` for flexibility.
5. **Test and Debug:** Verify operations for correctness and efficiency.

Syntax Table:

SL No	Function	Syntax/Example	Description
1	Apply Activation Function	`F.relu(input)`	Applies ReLU activation to input tensor.
2	Perform Linear Transformation	`F.linear(input, weight, bias)`	Implements a stateless fully connected layer.
3	Apply Convolution	`F.conv2d(input, weight, bias)`	Performs 2D convolution on input tensor.
4	Normalize Tensor	`F.batch_norm(input, running_mean, running_var)`	Normalizes input across a batch.
5	Create Custom Layer	Combine multiple `F.*` calls	Implements a custom layer using Functional API.

Syntax Explanation:

1. Apply Activation Function

What is Applying an Activation Function?

Activation functions introduce non-linearity into the model, enabling it to learn complex patterns. Using the Functional API, activations are applied directly to tensors without creating layers.

Syntax:

```
import torch.nn.functional as F
output = F.relu(input)
```

Detailed Explanation:

- **Purpose:** Transforms input tensors by applying non-linear functions element-wise.
- **Common Functions:**
  - `F.relu`: ReLU activation, sets negative values to zero.
  - `F.sigmoid`: Maps values to the range [0, 1].
  - `F.tanh`: Maps values to the range [-1, 1].

- **Behavior:**
  - o Processes each element independently.
  - o Outputs a tensor of the same shape as the input.

Example:

```
import torch
import torch.nn.functional as F
input_tensor = torch.tensor([[-1.0, 2.0], [0.0, -3.0]])
output = F.relu(input_tensor)
print(output)
```

Example Explanation:

- Applies ReLU to the input tensor.
- Sets all negative values to zero, producing `tensor([[0.0, 2.0], [0.0, 0.0]])`.

2. Perform Linear Transformation

What is a Linear Transformation?

A linear transformation maps input features to output features using learned weights and biases. The Functional API performs this transformation directly using tensors.

Syntax:

```
output = F.linear(input, weight, bias)
```

Detailed Explanation:

- **Purpose:** Implements a stateless fully connected layer for tasks like classification and regression.
- **Parameters:**
  - o input: Input tensor of shape `[batch_size, in_features]`.
  - o weight: Weight matrix of shape `[out_features, in_features]`.
  - o bias: Optional bias tensor of shape `[out_features]`.
- **Behavior:**
  - o Computes the dot product between input and weight.T.
  - o Adds bias to the result if provided.
- **Output:** A tensor of shape `[batch_size, out_features]`.

Example:
```
input = torch.randn(32, 128)    # Batch of 32 samples
with 128 features
weight = torch.randn(64, 128)   # Maps 128 features to
64 outputs
bias = torch.randn(64)
output = F.linear(input, weight, bias)
print(output.shape)
```
Example Explanation:
- Computes a linear transformation mapping 128 input features to 64 output features.
- Outputs a tensor of shape [32, 64].

3. Apply Convolution
What is Applying a Convolution?
Convolution operations extract spatial features from input data, commonly used in image and video processing.
Syntax:
```
output = F.conv2d(input, weight, bias)
```
Detailed Explanation:
- **Purpose:** Applies 2D convolution to extract spatial features like edges or textures.
- **Parameters:**
  - input: Input tensor of shape [batch_size, in_channels, height, width].
  - weight: Convolution filter weights of shape [out_channels, in_channels, kernel_height, kernel_width].
  - bias: Optional bias tensor of shape [out_channels].
- **Behavior:**
  - Slides the filter over the input tensor.
  - Computes element-wise products and sums them up.
- **Output:** Feature maps with reduced spatial dimensions, depending on stride and padding.

Example:
```
input = torch.randn(8, 3, 32, 32)    # Batch of 8 RGB
images (3 channels, 32x32 pixels)
weight = torch.randn(16, 3, 3, 3)    # 16 filters, 3x3
kernel size
bias = torch.randn(16)
output = F.conv2d(input, weight, bias)
print(output.shape)
```
Example Explanation:
- Applies 16 filters to a batch of 8 RGB images.
- Outputs feature maps of shape `[8, 16, 30, 30]`.

4. Normalize Tensor

What is Tensor Normalization?

Normalization ensures stable training by standardizing tensor values across a batch or feature dimension.

Syntax:
```
output = F.batch_norm(input, running_mean, running_var)
```
Detailed Explanation:
- **Purpose:** Normalizes the input tensor to improve convergence and stability.
- **Parameters:**
  - input: Input tensor of shape `[batch_size, num_features, ...]`.
  - running_mean: Running mean for each feature.
  - running_var: Running variance for each feature.
- **Behavior:**
  - Normalizes each feature as `(input - mean) / sqrt(variance + epsilon)`.
  - Applies learned scale and shift parameters if provided.
- **Output:** Normalized tensor with the same shape as the input.

Example:
```
input = torch.randn(16, 32)    # Batch of 16 samples with
32 features each
running_mean = torch.zeros(32)
running_var = torch.ones(32)
```

```
output = F.batch_norm(input, running_mean, running_var,
training=True)
print(output.shape)
```
Example Explanation:

- Normalizes a batch of 16 samples with 32 features each.
- Outputs a tensor of the same shape as the input.

5. Create Custom Layer
What is Creating a Custom Layer?

Custom layers combine multiple Functional API operations to define unique transformations or computations.

Syntax:
```
class CustomLayer(nn.Module):
    def __init__(self):
        super(CustomLayer, self).__init__()
    def forward(self, input):
        pass
```
Detailed Explanation:

- **Purpose:** Encapsulates custom logic for reuse in models.
- **Components:**
  - Combine F.* operations within the forward method.
  - Define initialization parameters if necessary.
- **Output:** A reusable layer implemented with Functional API operations.

Example:
```
class CustomLayer(nn.Module):
    def __init__(self):
        super(CustomLayer, self).__init__()
    def forward(self, input):
        x = F.linear(input, torch.randn(64, 128),
torch.randn(64))
        x = F.relu(x)
        return x
```
Example Explanation:

- Combines a linear transformation and ReLU activation in a custom layer.

- Processes input tensors and returns transformed outputs.

Real-Life Project:

Project Name: Custom Feature Extractor with Functional API
Project Goal:

Build a custom feature extractor using the Functional API to preprocess image data for a classification task.

Code for This Project:
```python
import torch
import torch.nn as nn
import torch.nn.functional as F
class FeatureExtractor(nn.Module):
    def __init__(self):
        super(FeatureExtractor, self).__init__()

    def forward(self, input):
        x = F.conv2d(input, torch.randn(16, 3, 3, 3),
bias=None)
        x = F.relu(x)
        x = F.batch_norm(x, torch.zeros(16),
torch.ones(16), training=True)
        x = F.max_pool2d(x, kernel_size=2)
        return x

# Example usage
input = torch.randn(8, 3, 32, 32)  # Batch of 8 RGB
images
model = FeatureExtractor()
output = model(input)
print(output.shape)
```
Expected Output:
- Processes 8 RGB images through the custom feature extractor.
- Outputs feature maps with reduced spatial dimensions, depending on the pooling layer configuration.

Chapter - 22 Distributed Training with PyTorch

Distributed training is an essential technique for scaling deep learning models across multiple devices or machines, enabling faster training on large datasets. PyTorch provides built-in support for distributed training via the `torch.distributed` package, allowing efficient communication and synchronization between processes. This chapter covers key concepts, tools, and strategies for implementing distributed training with PyTorch.

Key Characteristics of Distributed Training:

- **Scalability:** Utilizes multiple GPUs or machines to train models faster.
- **Efficiency:** Reduces training time by parallelizing data processing and model updates.
- **Flexibility:** Supports various training paradigms, including data parallelism and model parallelism.
- **Interoperability:** Works seamlessly with PyTorch's existing modules and APIs.
- **Fault Tolerance:** Provides mechanisms to handle process failures during training.

Steps to Implement Distributed Training:

1. **Initialize the Process Group:** Set up communication between distributed processes.
2. **Prepare the Model and Data:** Wrap the model and data loader for distributed training.
3. **Synchronize Gradients:** Use distributed optimizers or gradient reduction techniques.
4. **Run Training Loop:** Train the model across devices or nodes.
5. **Handle Synchronization:** Ensure proper initialization and synchronization of parameters.

Syntax Table:

SL No	Function	Syntax/Example	Description
1	Initialize Process Group	`torch.distributed.init_process_group(backend)`	Sets up the communication backend for distributed training.
2	Wrap Model	`torch.nn.parallel.DistributedDataParallel(model)`	Wraps the model for gradient synchronization.
3	Set Up Distributed Sampler	`torch.utils.data.distributed.DistributedSampler(dataset)`	Splits data across processes.
4	Synchronize Gradients	`optimizer.step()`	Updates model parameters across processes.
5	Launch Training Processes	`torch.multiprocessing.spawn(train_fn, args)`	Spawns multiple processes for distributed training.

Syntax Explanation:

1. Initialize Process Group
What is Initializing the Process Group?
The process group handles communication between distributed processes, enabling coordination and data sharing during training.
Syntax:
```
import torch.distributed as dist
dist.init_process_group(backend="nccl",
init_method="env://", world_size=4, rank=0)
```
Detailed Explanation:
- **Purpose:** Establishes the communication backend for distributed processes.
- **Parameters:**
    - backend: Specifies the communication backend ("nccl" for GPUs, "gloo" for CPUs).

- o   init_method: URL specifying initialization method (e.g., "env://" for environment variables).
- o   world_size: Total number of processes participating in training.
- o   rank: Rank of the current process.
- **Output:** Sets up the distributed environment for training.

Example:

```
import torch.distributed as dist
dist.init_process_group(backend="nccl",
init_method="env://", world_size=4, rank=0)
print("Process group initialized.")
```

Example Explanation:

- Initializes a distributed process group using the NCCL backend.
- Assumes 4 processes are involved in training.

2. Wrap Model

What is Wrapping the Model?

Wrapping the model ensures that gradients are synchronized across all processes during backpropagation.

Syntax:

```
from torch.nn.parallel import DistributedDataParallel
model = DistributedDataParallel(model)
```

Detailed Explanation:

- **Purpose:** Enables automatic gradient synchronization between distributed processes.
- **Parameters:**
  - o   model: The PyTorch model to wrap.
- **Behavior:**
  - o   Broadcasts initial model parameters to all processes.
  - o   Synchronizes gradients during the backward pass.
- **Output:** A distributed version of the model.

Example:

```
from torch.nn.parallel import DistributedDataParallel
model = DistributedDataParallel(model)
output = model(input)
```

Example Explanation:
- Wraps the model for distributed training.
- Allows seamless forward and backward passes across processes.

3. Set Up Distributed Sampler
What is a Distributed Sampler?
A distributed sampler divides the dataset into non-overlapping chunks for each process, ensuring efficient parallel data loading.
Syntax:
```
from torch.utils.data.distributed import
DistributedSampler
sampler = DistributedSampler(dataset)
data_loader = DataLoader(dataset, sampler=sampler)
```
Detailed Explanation:
- **Purpose:** Ensures each process works on a unique subset of data.
- **Parameters:**
  - dataset: The dataset to sample from.
  - num_replicas: Total number of processes (optional).
  - rank: Rank of the current process (optional).
- **Output:** A sampler object for distributed data loading.

Example:
```
sampler = DistributedSampler(dataset)
data_loader = DataLoader(dataset, sampler=sampler,
batch_size=32)
```
Example Explanation:
- Creates a data loader that distributes batches across processes.
- Ensures no overlap in data between processes.

4. Synchronize Gradients
What is Gradient Synchronization?
Synchronizing gradients ensures that updates to model parameters are consistent across all processes.
Syntax:
```
optimizer.step()
```
Detailed Explanation:
- **Purpose:** Updates model parameters based on synchronized

gradients.
- **Behavior:**
  - o   Each process computes local gradients.
  - o   Gradients are averaged across all processes before applying updates.
- **Output:** Updated model parameters.

Example:
```
loss.backward()  # Compute gradients
optimizer.step()  # Apply synchronized updates
```
Example Explanation:
- Backpropagates loss to compute gradients.
- Updates parameters using gradients averaged across processes.

5. Launch Training Processes
What is Launching Training Processes?
Launching training processes involves starting multiple worker processes, each responsible for a subset of the distributed training.
Syntax:
```
import torch.multiprocessing as mp
mp.spawn(train_fn, args=(world_size,),
nprocs=world_size, join=True)
```
Detailed Explanation:
- **Purpose:** Starts multiple processes for distributed training.
- **Parameters:**
  - o   train_fn: Function defining the training logic.
  - o   args: Arguments passed to the training function.
  - o   nprocs: Number of processes to spawn.
- **Output:** Parallel execution of training logic.

Example:
```
def train_fn(rank, world_size):
    dist.init_process_group(backend="nccl",
world_size=world_size, rank=rank)
    # Training logic here
mp.spawn(train_fn, args=(4,), nprocs=4, join=True)
```
Example Explanation:
- Spawns 4 processes for distributed training.

- Each process initializes the distributed environment and runs the training logic.

Real-Life Project:

Project Name: Distributed Image Classification
Project Goal: Train an image classification model on a large dataset using multiple GPUs with distributed training.
Code for This Project:

```
import torch
import torch.distributed as dist
import torch.multiprocessing as mp
from torch.nn.parallel import DistributedDataParallel
from torch.utils.data import DataLoader,
DistributedSampler
from torchvision import datasets, transforms
from torch import nn, optim

def train_fn(rank, world_size):
    dist.init_process_group(backend="nccl",
init_method="env://", world_size=world_size, rank=rank)

    transform = transforms.ToTensor()
    dataset = datasets.CIFAR10(root="data", train=True,
transform=transform, download=True)
    sampler = DistributedSampler(dataset,
num_replicas=world_size, rank=rank)
    data_loader = DataLoader(dataset, sampler=sampler,
batch_size=64)

    model = nn.Sequential(
        nn.Flatten(),
        nn.Linear(32 * 32 * 3, 128),
        nn.ReLU(),
        nn.Linear(128, 10)
    ).to(rank)
    model = DistributedDataParallel(model,
```

```python
        device_ids=[rank])
    criterion = nn.CrossEntropyLoss()
    optimizer = optim.SGD(model.parameters(), lr=0.01)
    for epoch in range(5):
        sampler.set_epoch(epoch)
        for images, labels in data_loader:
            images, labels = images.to(rank),
labels.to(rank)
            optimizer.zero_grad()
            outputs = model(images)
            loss = criterion(outputs, labels)
            loss.backward()
            optimizer.step()

        if rank == 0:
            print(f"Epoch {epoch+1}, Loss:
{loss.item():.4f}")

def main():
    world_size = 4
    mp.spawn(train_fn, args=(world_size,),
nprocs=world_size, join=True)
if __name__ == "__main__":
    main()
```

Expected Output:

- Training loss decreases over epochs.
- The model trains efficiently across 4 GPUs, leveraging distributed computation.

Chapter - 23 Handling Large Models with Model Parallelism

Model parallelism is a technique used to handle large models that exceed the memory capacity of a single GPU by splitting the model across multiple GPUs. This allows deep learning practitioners to train models with large parameter counts or memory-intensive architectures. PyTorch provides tools for implementing model parallelism, enabling efficient computation and memory utilization.

Key Characteristics of Model Parallelism:

- **Scalability:** Distributes model components across multiple devices.
- **Memory Efficiency:** Splits model weights and activations to fit within GPU memory constraints.
- **Flexibility:** Supports both manual and automated model partitioning.
- **Interoperability:** Works seamlessly with PyTorch's data parallelism and distributed training.
- **Customizability:** Allows granular control over model and data placement.

Steps to Implement Model Parallelism:

1. **Identify Model Components:** Determine which parts of the model to distribute across devices.
2. **Assign Components to GPUs:** Place layers or sub-models on specific GPUs using `.to(device)`.
3. **Manage Data Flow:** Ensure intermediate outputs are transferred between GPUs as needed.
4. **Train the Model:** Implement the training loop, taking care to synchronize GPU computations.
5. **Optimize for Performance:** Minimize GPU communication overhead and memory usage.

Syntax Table:

SL No	Function	Syntax/Example	Description
1	Move Model to GPU	`layer.to(device)`	Places a model or layer on a specific GPU.
2	Split Model Across GPUs	`submodel1.to("cuda:0"), submodel2.to("cuda:1")`	Distributes model components across GPUs.
3	Transfer Data Between GPUs	`output = output.to("cuda:1")`	Moves data from one GPU to another.
4	Manage Gradients	`optimizer.step()`	Ensures gradients are computed across devices.
5	Handle Multi-GPU Training	Combine with `DistributedDataParallel`	Scales model parallelism to multiple nodes.

Syntax Explanation:

1. Move Model to GPU

What is Moving a Model to a GPU?

Moving a model or layer to a specific GPU allows computations to leverage the GPU's memory and processing power.

Syntax:

```
layer = nn.Linear(512, 256)
device = torch.device("cuda:0")
layer.to(device)
```

Detailed Explanation:

- **Purpose:** Allocates model parameters and buffers to a specific GPU.
- **Parameters:**
    - device: Target device, such as `"cuda:0"` or `"cuda:1"`.

- **Behavior:**
  - o Ensures all computations and storage for the layer occur on the specified GPU.
- **Output:** A layer object now residing on the target GPU.

Example:
```
layer = nn.Linear(512, 256)
layer = layer.to("cuda:0")
data = torch.randn(64, 512).to("cuda:0")
output = layer(data)
print(output.device)
```
Example Explanation:
- Allocates a fully connected layer and input tensor to GPU 0.
- Computes the forward pass entirely on GPU 0.

2. Split Model Across GPUs

What is Splitting a Model Across GPUs?

Splitting a model involves assigning different layers or sub-models to separate GPUs, enabling memory and computation to be distributed.

Syntax:
```
submodel1 = nn.Linear(512, 256).to("cuda:0")
submodel2 = nn.Linear(256, 128).to("cuda:1")
```
Detailed Explanation:
- **Purpose:** Distributes model components to balance memory usage and computation load.
- **Parameters:**
  - o `submodel1`, `submodel2`: Separate layers or sub-models assigned to different GPUs.
- **Behavior:**
  - o Data output from one GPU must be transferred to the next GPU for further processing.
- **Output:** Sub-models placed on specific GPUs.

Example:
```
submodel1 = nn.Linear(512, 256).to("cuda:0")
submodel2 = nn.Linear(256, 128).to("cuda:1")
data = torch.randn(64, 512).to("cuda:0")
output = submodel1(data)
```

```
output = output.to("cuda:1")
output = submodel2(output)
print(output.device)
```
Example Explanation:

- Splits computation between two GPUs.
- Moves intermediate results from GPU 0 to GPU 1 for further processing.

3. Transfer Data Between GPUs
What is Transferring Data Between GPUs?
Transferring data ensures that intermediate results produced by one GPU are available for computation on another GPU.

Syntax:
```
output = output.to("cuda:1")
```
Detailed Explanation:

- **Purpose:** Moves tensors between GPUs to continue the computation pipeline.
- **Parameters:**
    - output: Tensor to be transferred.
    - "cuda:1": Target GPU for the tensor.
- **Behavior:**
    - Transfers tensor data over the PCIe bus or NVLink (if available).
    - Introduces communication overhead, which should be minimized.
- **Output:** Tensor now residing on the target GPU.

Example:
```
input = torch.randn(64, 512).to("cuda:0")
output = input.to("cuda:1")
print(output.device)
```
Example Explanation:

- Transfers a tensor from GPU 0 to GPU 1.
- Ensures data is accessible for computations on GPU 1.

4. Manage Gradients

What is Managing Gradients?

Managing gradients ensures that model updates occur correctly across GPUs, even when layers are split between devices.

Syntax:

```
optimizer.step()
```

Detailed Explanation:

- **Purpose:** Updates model parameters based on computed gradients.
- **Behavior:**
    - Computes gradients locally on each GPU.
    - Aggregates or synchronizes gradients if needed.
- **Output:** Updated model parameters across all GPUs.

Example:

```
loss.backward()  # Compute gradients
optimizer.step()  # Apply updates
```

Example Explanation:

- Backpropagates loss to compute gradients.
- Updates parameters for all parts of the distributed model.

5. Handle Multi-GPU Training

What is Handling Multi-GPU Training?

Combining model parallelism with `DistributedDataParallel` allows efficient scaling to multiple nodes and GPUs.

Syntax:

```
from torch.nn.parallel import DistributedDataParallel
model = DistributedDataParallel(model)
```

Detailed Explanation:

- **Purpose:** Ensures synchronization of gradients and updates across GPUs and nodes.
- **Parameters:**
    - `model`: The model or sub-model to wrap.
- **Behavior:**
    - Automatically synchronizes gradients during backpropagation.
- **Output:** A model configured for distributed training.

Example:

```
from torch.nn.parallel import DistributedDataParallel
model = nn.Linear(512, 256).to("cuda:0")
model = DistributedDataParallel(model, device_ids=[0])
```

Example Explanation:

- Wraps a model for distributed training across GPUs.
- Ensures consistent gradient updates across processes.

Real-Life Project:

Project Name: Large-Scale Language Model Training with Model
Parallelism

Project Goal: Train a transformer-based language model with billions of
parameters using model parallelism.

Code for This Project:

```
import torch
import torch.nn as nn
from torch.nn.parallel import DistributedDataParallel
class LargeModel(nn.Module):
    def __init__(self):
        super(LargeModel, self).__init__()
        self.layer1 = nn.Linear(1024,
2048).to("cuda:0")
        self.layer2 = nn.Linear(2048,
1024).to("cuda:1")

    def forward(self, x):
        x = self.layer1(x)
        x = x.to("cuda:1")
        x = self.layer2(x)
        return x

# Initialize model
model = LargeModel()

# Wrap model with DistributedDataParallel
model = DistributedDataParallel(model, device_ids=[0,
```

```
1])

# Training loop
optimizer = torch.optim.SGD(model.parameters(),
lr=0.01)
loss_fn = nn.MSELoss()
data = torch.randn(64, 1024).to("cuda:0")
labels = torch.randn(64, 1024).to("cuda:1")

for epoch in range(5):
    optimizer.zero_grad()
    outputs = model(data)
    loss = loss_fn(outputs, labels)
    loss.backward()
    optimizer.step()
    print(f"Epoch {epoch+1}, Loss: {loss.item():.4f}")
```
Expected Output:
- Training loss decreases over epochs.
- Model components distributed across GPUs train collaboratively, leveraging model parallelism.

Chapter - 24 Mixed Precision Training for Performance Optimization

Mixed precision training is a technique that uses both 32-bit (single precision) and 16-bit (half precision) floating-point arithmetic to accelerate deep learning training while reducing memory consumption. PyTorch provides native support for mixed precision training through the `torch.cuda.amp` module, making it easier to achieve faster training times without sacrificing model accuracy. This chapter explains the concepts, benefits, and implementation of mixed precision training.

Key Characteristics of Mixed Precision Training:
- **Speed:** Leverages faster 16-bit operations on GPUs, especially with Tensor Cores on NVIDIA GPUs.
- **Memory Efficiency:** Reduces memory usage, allowing larger batch sizes or models.
- **Accuracy:** Maintains model accuracy by selectively using 32-bit precision for critical operations.
- **Compatibility:** Works seamlessly with most PyTorch layers and optimizers.

Steps to Implement Mixed Precision Training:
1. **Enable Automatic Mixed Precision (AMP):** Use `torch.cuda.amp.autocast` to automatically cast operations to appropriate precision.
2. **Use Gradient Scaling:** Apply `GradScaler` to prevent underflow in gradients.
3. **Modify Training Loop:** Integrate AMP and gradient scaling into the training process.
4. **Test Model Accuracy:** Verify that mixed precision training does not degrade model performance.

Syntax Table:

SL No	Function	Syntax/Example	Description
1	Enable Mixed Precision	`with torch.cuda.amp.a utocast():`	Enables mixed precision for specific operations.
2	Initialize GradScaler	`scaler = torch.cuda.amp.G radScaler()`	Initializes gradient scaling to handle underflow.
3	Scale Gradients	`scaler.scale(los s).backward()`	Scales loss to prevent gradient underflow.
4	Update Optimizer	`scaler.step(opti mizer)`	Applies scaled gradients to the optimizer.
5	Unscale Gradients	`scaler.unscale_( optimizer)`	Unscales gradients for debugging or clipping.

Syntax Explanation:

1. Enable Mixed Precision
What is Enabling Mixed Precision?
Enabling mixed precision allows specific operations to run in 16-bit precision, while others remain in 32-bit precision when necessary for accuracy.
Syntax:
```
with torch.cuda.amp.autocast():
    output = model(input)
    loss = loss_fn(output, target)
```
Detailed Explanation:
- **Purpose:** Automatically casts operations to the appropriate precision based on hardware capabilities.
- **Parameters:** None required; the context manager handles casting internally.
- **Behavior:**
    o Most operations are performed in 16-bit precision.
    o Operations that require higher precision (e.g., softmax) are automatically performed in 32-bit.

- **Output:** Results computed with mixed precision, reducing memory usage and improving speed.

Example:
```
with torch.cuda.amp.autocast():
    output = model(input)
    loss = loss_fn(output, target)
```
Example Explanation:
- Computes the forward pass with mixed precision.
- Reduces memory usage for intermediate tensors.

2. Initialize GradScaler
What is Initializing GradScaler?
Gradient scaling prevents underflow in gradients during backpropagation when using 16-bit precision.
Syntax:
```
scaler = torch.cuda.amp.GradScaler()
```
Detailed Explanation:
- **Purpose:** Dynamically scales gradients to maintain numerical stability.
- **Behavior:**
  - Scales the loss value before backpropagation.
  - Automatically adjusts the scaling factor based on gradient values.
- **Output:** A GradScaler object for managing scaling during training.

Example:
```
scaler = torch.cuda.amp.GradScaler()
```
Example Explanation:
- Initializes a gradient scaler for mixed precision training.
- Ensures stable updates during optimization.

3. Scale Gradients
What is Scaling Gradients?
Scaling gradients amplifies their values to avoid underflow during 16-bit backpropagation.

Syntax:

```
scaler.scale(loss).backward()
```

Detailed Explanation:

- **Purpose:** Prevents gradients from becoming too small to represent in 16-bit precision.
- **Parameters:**
    - `loss`: The computed loss value.
- **Behavior:**
    - Multiplies the loss by a scaling factor before calling `.backward()`.
    - Scales down gradients during optimization.
- **Output:** Scaled gradients for backpropagation.

Example:

```
scaler.scale(loss).backward()
```

Example Explanation:

- Computes gradients with a scaled loss value.
- Avoids numerical instability in gradient calculations.

4. Update Optimizer

What is Updating the Optimizer?

Updating the optimizer applies the scaled gradients to the model parameters.

Syntax:

```
scaler.step(optimizer)
```

Detailed Explanation:

- **Purpose:** Ensures the optimizer updates parameters using correctly scaled gradients.
- **Parameters:**
    - `optimizer`: The PyTorch optimizer managing parameter updates.
- **Behavior:**
    - Applies gradients to update model parameters.
    - Automatically skips updates if gradients contain NaN or Inf values.
- **Output:** Updated model parameters.

Example:
```
scaler.step(optimizer)
scaler.update()
```
Example Explanation:
- Applies scaled gradients to the optimizer.
- Adjusts the scaling factor for subsequent iterations.

5. Unscale Gradients
What is Unscaling Gradients?
Unscaling gradients reverts them to their original values for debugging or clipping purposes.
Syntax:
```
scaler.unscale_(optimizer)
```
Detailed Explanation:
- **Purpose:** Allows inspection or modification of gradients before applying updates.
- **Parameters:**
  - optimizer: The optimizer managing the gradients.
- **Behavior:**
  - Converts scaled gradients back to their original scale.
  - Enables gradient clipping or inspection for stability.
- **Output:** Unscaled gradients ready for debugging or processing.

Example:
```
scaler.unscale_(optimizer)
torch.nn.utils.clip_grad_norm_(model.parameters(),
max_norm=1.0)
```
Example Explanation:
- Unscales gradients before applying gradient clipping.
- Prevents excessively large updates to model parameters.

Real-Life Project:

Project Name: Image Classification with Mixed Precision Training
Project Goal: Train a ResNet model on the CIFAR-10 dataset using mixed precision to reduce memory usage and accelerate training.
Code for This Project:

```python
import torch
import torch.nn as nn
import torch.optim as optim
from torch.cuda.amp import autocast, GradScaler
from torchvision import datasets, transforms
from torchvision.models import resnet18

# Data preparation
transform = transforms.Compose([
    transforms.ToTensor(),
    transforms.Normalize((0.5,), (0.5,))
])
train_dataset = datasets.CIFAR10(root='data',
train=True, transform=transform, download=True)
train_loader =
torch.utils.data.DataLoader(train_dataset,
batch_size=64, shuffle=True)

# Model, loss, and optimizer
model = resnet18().cuda()
criterion = nn.CrossEntropyLoss()
optimizer = optim.SGD(model.parameters(), lr=0.01)
scaler = GradScaler()

# Training loop
for epoch in range(5):
    for inputs, targets in train_loader:
        inputs, targets = inputs.cuda(), targets.cuda()

        # Forward pass with mixed precision
        with autocast():
            outputs = model(inputs)
            loss = criterion(outputs, targets)

        # Backward pass and optimization
        scaler.scale(loss).backward()
        scaler.step(optimizer)
```

```
        scaler.update()
    print(f"Epoch {epoch+1}, Loss: {loss.item():.4f}")
print("Training complete.")
```

Expected Output:
- Training loss decreases over epochs.
- The model trains faster and uses less memory compared to full 32-bit precision training.

Chapter - 25 Model Quantization and Pruning

Model quantization and pruning are techniques for optimizing deep learning models by reducing their size and computational complexity. Quantization reduces the precision of model weights and activations, while pruning removes redundant parameters or connections. These methods are essential for deploying models on resource-constrained devices, such as mobile phones or edge devices, without sacrificing significant performance. This chapter explores how to implement and leverage these techniques in PyTorch.

Key Characteristics of Quantization and Pruning:

- **Quantization:**
    - Converts 32-bit floating-point weights to lower precision (e.g., 8-bit integers).
    - Reduces model size and accelerates inference on hardware supporting low precision.

- **Pruning:**
    - Removes unimportant parameters based on their contribution to the model.
    - Maintains accuracy while decreasing model size and complexity.

- **Compatibility:** Works with pre-trained models or during training.
- **Efficiency:** Enables real-time inference on constrained devices.

Steps to Implement Quantization:

1. **Choose Quantization Type:** Select from dynamic, static, or quantization-aware training (QAT).
2. **Prepare the Model:** Use PyTorch's quantization utilities to prepare the model for quantization.
3. **Apply Quantization:** Perform dynamic, static, or QAT quantization on the model.
4. **Evaluate Performance:** Verify accuracy and measure latency improvements.

Steps to Implement Pruning:

1. **Choose Pruning Method:** Select from unstructured, structured, or global pruning.

2. **Apply Pruning:** Use PyTorch's pruning functions to remove parameters.
3. **Fine-Tune the Model:** Retrain the pruned model to recover accuracy.
4. **Save the Model:** Export the pruned model for deployment.

Syntax Table:

SL NO	Function	Syntax/Example	Description
1	Apply Dynamic Quantization	`torch.quantization.quantize_dynamic(model)`	Dynamically quantizes weights during inference.
2	Apply Static Quantization	`torch.quantization.prepare(model)`	Prepares the model for static quantization.
3	Perform Quantization-Aware Training	`torch.quantization.prepare_qat(model)`	Simulates quantization effects during training.
4	Apply Unstructured Pruning	`torch.nn.utils.prune.random_unstructured(layer, amount)`	Removes random connections from the layer.
5	Fine-Tune Pruned Model	`model.train()`	Retrains the model to recover accuracy.

Syntax Explanation:
1. Apply Dynamic Quantization
What is Dynamic Quantization?
Dynamic quantization converts weights to lower precision (e.g., 8-bit integers) during inference, improving latency without requiring full retraining.
Syntax:
```
import torch from torch.quantization import quantize_dynamic
quantized_model = quantize_dynamic(model, {torch.nn.Linear}, dtype=torch.qint8)
```

Detailed Explanation:
- **Purpose:** Reduces computational cost and memory usage during inference.
- **Parameters:**
  - `model`: The pre-trained PyTorch model to quantize.
  - `modules`: Specifies which layers to quantize (e.g., `torch.nn.Linear`).
  - `dtype`: Specifies the quantization data type (e.g., `torch.qint8`).
- **Behavior:**
  - Quantizes weights dynamically during inference.
  - Leaves activations in full precision.
- **Output:** A quantized version of the model.

Example:
```
quantized_model = quantize_dynamic(model,
{torch.nn.Linear}, dtype=torch.qint8)
print(quantized_model)
```

Example Explanation:
- Converts linear layers of a model to 8-bit precision.
- Maintains compatibility with full-precision inputs.

2. Apply Static Quantization

What is Static Quantization?

Static quantization converts weights and activations to lower precision, improving both inference speed and memory efficiency.

Syntax:
```
import torch
from torch.quantization import prepare, convert
model.eval()
model = prepare(model)
model = convert(model)
```

Detailed Explanation:
- **Purpose:** Quantizes both weights and activations for maximum efficiency.
- **Steps:**
  - `prepare`: Prepares the model by adding observers to

collect activation statistics.

- o convert: Finalizes the quantization using collected statistics.
- **Output:** A fully quantized model.

Example:

```
model = prepare(model)
model = convert(model)
print(model)
```

Example Explanation:

- Prepares and converts the model for static quantization.
- Collects activation statistics during a calibration phase.

3. Perform Quantization-Aware Training

What is Quantization-Aware Training?

Quantization-aware training (QAT) simulates quantization during training to minimize accuracy loss.

Syntax:

```
from torch.quantization import prepare_qat, convert
model.train()
model = prepare_qat(model)
# Train the model here
model = convert(model)
```

Detailed Explanation:

- **Purpose:** Incorporates quantization effects during training to ensure accuracy.
- **Steps:**
  - o prepare_qat: Simulates quantization during training.
  - o Train the model with the standard PyTorch training loop.
  - o convert: Finalizes the quantization process.
- **Output:** A quantized model trained for high accuracy.

Example:

```
model = prepare_qat(model)
# Train the model
model = convert(model)
```

Example Explanation:

- Simulates quantization during training to ensure robustness.
- Converts the trained model to a quantized version.

4. Apply Unstructured Pruning

What is Unstructured Pruning?

Unstructured pruning removes individual weights within a layer based on their magnitude or randomly.

Syntax:

```
from torch.nn.utils import prune
prune.random_unstructured(layer, name='weight',
amount=0.2)
```

Detailed Explanation:

- **Purpose:** Reduces the number of parameters in a model to improve efficiency.
- **Parameters:**
    - `layer`: The layer to prune (e.g., `torch.nn.Linear`).
    - `name`: Specifies the parameter to prune (e.g., `'weight'`).
    - `amount`: Fraction of connections to prune (e.g., `0.2` for 20%).
- **Behavior:**
    - Removes connections based on the specified method (e.g., random or magnitude).
    - Creates a sparse version of the weights.
- **Output:** A pruned version of the layer.

Example:

```
prune.random_unstructured(layer, name='weight',
amount=0.2)
print(layer.weight)
```

Example Explanation:

- Randomly prunes 20% of the weights in the specified layer.
- Leaves the remaining weights unchanged.

5. Fine-Tune Pruned Model

What is Fine-Tuning a Pruned Model?

Fine-tuning a pruned model retrains it to recover accuracy lost during pruning.

Syntax:

```
model.train()
for epoch in range(epochs):
    # Training loop
    optimizer.step()
```

Detailed Explanation:

- **Purpose:** Restores the model's accuracy after pruning.
- **Steps:**
  - Train the model as usual with pruned weights.
  - Adjust hyperparameters as needed to stabilize training.
- **Output:** A fine-tuned, efficient model.

Example:

```
for epoch in range(5):
    optimizer.zero_grad()
    output = model(data)
    loss = loss_fn(output, target)
    loss.backward()
    optimizer.step()
```

Example Explanation:

- Retrains the pruned model over 5 epochs.
- Restores performance close to the original unpruned model.

Real-Life Project:

Project Name: Deployable Image Classifier with Quantization and Pruning
Project Goal: Optimize a ResNet model for deployment on mobile devices using quantization and pruning.

Code for This Project:

```
import torch
import torch.nn as nn
import torch.optim as optim
from torchvision.models import resnet18
from torch.nn.utils import prune
from torch.quantization import quantize_dynamic
```

```python
# Load pre-trained model
model = resnet18(pretrained=True)
model.eval()

# Apply pruning
for name, module in model.named_modules():
    if isinstance(module, nn.Linear):
        prune.l1_unstructured(module, name='weight',
amount=0.2)

# Apply dynamic quantization
quantized_model = quantize_dynamic(model, {nn.Linear},
dtype=torch.qint8)

# Fine-tune the pruned model
optimizer = optim.SGD(quantized_model.parameters(),
lr=0.01)
loss_fn = nn.CrossEntropyLoss()

data = torch.randn(16, 3, 224, 224)  # Dummy input
labels = torch.randint(0, 1000, (16,))

for epoch in range(5):
    optimizer.zero_grad()
    output = quantized_model(data)
    loss = loss_fn(output, labels)
    loss.backward()
    optimizer.step()

    print(f"Epoch {epoch+1}, Loss: {loss.item():.4f}")
```

Expected Output:
- Training loss decreases over epochs.
- The quantized and pruned model retains competitive accuracy while being efficient for deployment.

Chapter - 26 PyTorch's Computer Vision Libraries

PyTorch provides a rich ecosystem of computer vision libraries, including `torchvision`, to simplify the development of image processing and vision-based deep learning models. These libraries offer pre-trained models, datasets, transformations, and utilities to accelerate the implementation of tasks like classification, object detection, and segmentation. This chapter explores the key features and usage of PyTorch's computer vision libraries.

Key Characteristics of PyTorch's Computer Vision Libraries:

- **Pre-trained Models:** Access state-of-the-art models for tasks like classification, detection, and segmentation.
- **Datasets:** Simplified loading and preprocessing of popular datasets like CIFAR, ImageNet, and COCO.
- **Transforms:** Utilities for data augmentation and preprocessing.
- **Integration:** Seamlessly integrates with PyTorch's data loaders and model training pipeline.
- **Customizability:** Allows users to define custom datasets and augmentations.

Steps to Use PyTorch's Computer Vision Libraries:

1. **Import `torchvision`:** Access datasets, models, and transforms.
2. **Load Datasets:** Use built-in datasets or define custom datasets.
3. **Apply Transforms:** Preprocess data with augmentation techniques.
4. **Use Pre-trained Models:** Fine-tune or evaluate pre-trained models.
5. **Train and Evaluate:** Integrate with PyTorch's training and evaluation workflow.

Syntax Table:

SL No	Function	Syntax/Example	Description
1	Import torchvision	`import torchvision`	Imports PyTorch's computer vision library.
2	Load Dataset	`datasets.CIFAR10(root, train=True)`	Loads a dataset with optional preprocessing.
3	Apply Transformations	`transforms.Compose([...])`	Chains preprocessing and augmentation steps.
4	Load Pre-trained Model	`models.resnet18(pretrained=True)`	Loads a pre-trained ResNet model.
5	Perform Inference	`model(input)`	Runs a forward pass for prediction.

Syntax Explanation:

1. Import `torchvision`

What is Importing `torchvision`?
Importing `torchvision` provides access to its datasets, models, and transforms modules for computer vision tasks.
Syntax:
`import torchvision`
Detailed Explanation:
- **Purpose:** Grants access to a collection of tools for computer vision tasks.
- **Submodules:**
  - `torchvision.datasets`: For loading datasets.
  - `torchvision.transforms`: For data preprocessing and augmentation.
  - `torchvision.models`: For pre-trained deep learning models.

- **Behavior:**
  - Provides a consistent interface to access datasets, transformations, and models.
  - Streamlines the development of computer vision tasks by leveraging pre-built utilities.
- **Output:** Imports the `torchvision` library, enabling its functionalities.

Example:
```
import torchvision
from torchvision import datasets, transforms, models
```
Example Explanation:
- Imports `torchvision` and its key submodules for dataset loading, image transformations, and accessing pre-trained models.
- Prepares the environment for using `torchvision` functionalities in computer vision workflows.

2. Load Dataset

What is Loading a Dataset?
Loading a dataset retrieves image data for training or evaluation, with optional preprocessing steps for efficient model input preparation.

Syntax:
```
from torchvision import datasets
dataset = datasets.CIFAR10(root="data", train=True,
download=True, transform=transform)
```
Detailed Explanation:
- **Purpose:** Provides a convenient way to access and preprocess popular image datasets.
- **Parameters:**
  - `root`: Specifies the directory where the dataset will be stored or is already stored.
  - `train`: Boolean flag indicating whether to load the training split (`True`) or test split (`False`).
  - `download`: Downloads the dataset if it is not already present in the specified directory.

- o transform: Applies transformations such as resizing, cropping, or normalization to the dataset.
- **Behavior:**
  - o Loads the dataset into memory or prepares it for streaming via a data loader.
  - o Automatically handles dataset structure and preprocessing steps.
- **Output:** A dataset object compatible with PyTorch's DataLoader for batch processing.

Example:

```
transform = transforms.Compose([
    transforms.ToTensor(),
    transforms.Normalize((0.5,), (0.5,))
])
dataset = datasets.CIFAR10(root="data", train=True,
download=True, transform=transform)
```

Example Explanation:
- Applies transformations such as converting images to tensors and normalizing pixel values to have a mean of 0.5 and standard deviation of 0.5.
- Loads the CIFAR-10 training dataset, ensuring it is ready for model input.

3. Apply Transformations

What are Transformations?
Transformations preprocess and augment image data to improve model generalization and facilitate effective training.

Syntax:

```
from torchvision import transforms
transform = transforms.Compose([
    transforms.Resize(256),
    transforms.CenterCrop(224),
    transforms.ToTensor(),
    transforms.Normalize((0.5,), (0.5,))
])
```

Detailed Explanation:

- **Purpose:** Chains multiple preprocessing steps into a single pipeline for streamlined data preparation.
- **Common Transformations:**
    - `transforms.Resize`: Resizes input images to the specified dimensions.
    - `transforms.CenterCrop`: Crops the central region of the image to a specified size.
    - `transforms.ToTensor`: Converts image data from PIL format to PyTorch tensors, scaling pixel values to [0, 1].
    - `transforms.Normalize`: Normalizes image pixel values based on the specified mean and standard deviation for each channel.
- **Behavior:**
    - Applies transformations sequentially in the order they are defined.
    - Outputs processed tensors ready for model input.

Example:

```
transform = transforms.Compose([
    transforms.RandomHorizontalFlip(),
    transforms.RandomRotation(10),
    transforms.ToTensor()
])
```

Example Explanation:

- Applies random horizontal flipping and rotation to augment the dataset, improving model robustness.
- Converts images to PyTorch tensors, making them compatible with the training process.

4. Load Pre-trained Model

What is Loading a Pre-trained Model?

Pre-trained models provide a starting point for training or evaluation, offering weights optimized on large datasets such as ImageNet.

Syntax:

```
from torchvision import models
model = models.resnet18(pretrained=True)
```

Detailed Explanation:

- **Purpose:** Reduces training time by leveraging models already trained on large datasets.
- **Parameters:**
    - `pretrained`: If True, loads pre-trained weights for the model architecture.
- **Behavior:**
    - Allows fine-tuning by modifying the output layer for specific tasks.
    - Supports transfer learning by freezing certain layers.
- **Output:** A pre-trained model object ready for inference or fine-tuning.

Example:

```
model = models.resnet18(pretrained=True)
print(model)
```

Example Explanation:

- Instantiates a ResNet-18 model pre-trained on ImageNet.
- Prints the model architecture to inspect its layers and structure.

5. Perform Inference

What is Performing Inference?

Inference uses a trained or pre-trained model to make predictions on unseen data.

Syntax:

```
model.eval()
output = model(input)
```

Detailed Explanation:

- **Purpose:** Generates predictions from the model based on input data.
- **Steps:**
    - Switch the model to evaluation mode using

> model.eval() to disable dropout and batch
> normalization updates.
> ○ Pass the input tensor through the model.
- **Output:** Predictions, typically in the form of logits or probabilities for classification tasks.

Example:

```
input = torch.randn(1, 3, 224, 224)  # Dummy input
image with batch size 1
output = model(input)
print(output)
```

Example Explanation:
- Simulates an inference step with a randomly generated input image.
- Outputs the model's predictions, which can be interpreted as class probabilities or logits.

Real-Life Project:

Project Name: Image Classification with Pre-trained Models

Project Goal: Use a pre-trained ResNet model to classify images from the CIFAR-10 dataset.

Code for This Project:

```
import torch
from torchvision import datasets, transforms, models
from torch.utils.data import DataLoader

# Data preparation
transform = transforms.Compose([
    transforms.Resize(224),
    transforms.ToTensor(),
    transforms.Normalize((0.5,), (0.5,))
])

dataset = datasets.CIFAR10(root="data", train=False,
download=True, transform=transform)
data_loader = DataLoader(dataset, batch_size=32,
shuffle=False)
```

```python
# Load pre-trained model
model = models.resnet18(pretrained=True)
model.eval()

# Perform inference
for inputs, _ in data_loader:
    outputs = model(inputs)
    _, preds = torch.max(outputs, 1)
    print(preds)
```

Expected Output:

- Prints predicted class indices for batches of CIFAR-10 images.
- Demonstrates the use of a pre-trained model for inference.

Chapter - 27 Building Image Classification Models

Image classification is a fundamental task in computer vision, where the goal is to assign a label to an image from a predefined set of categories. PyTorch provides extensive tools and utilities to build, train, and evaluate image classification models. This chapter covers how to design and implement image classification models using PyTorch, from data preparation to evaluation.

Key Characteristics of Image Classification Models:
- **Versatility:** Supports both simple architectures and complex deep learning models.
- **Pre-trained Models:** Provides pre-trained models for transfer learning.
- **Customizability:** Allows users to define and train custom architectures.
- **Integration:** Seamlessly integrates with PyTorch's ecosystem for data handling and optimization.
- **Scalability:** Capable of handling datasets of varying sizes and complexities.

Steps to Build an Image Classification Model:
1. **Prepare the Dataset:** Load and preprocess image data.
2. **Define the Model:** Design or choose an architecture suitable for the task.
3. **Set Up the Training Pipeline:** Define the loss function, optimizer, and training loop.
4. **Train the Model:** Train the model on the dataset and monitor performance.
5. **Evaluate the Model:** Test the model on unseen data and measure accuracy.
6. **Fine-Tune and Save:** Fine-tune the model if needed and save it for deployment.

Syntax Table:

SL No	Function	Syntax/Example	Description
1	Load Dataset	`datasets.ImageFolder(root, transform)`	Loads image data from a folder structure.
2	Define Model	`nn.Sequential(*layers)`	Constructs a model architecture.
3	Compile Training Components	`optimizer = torch.optim.SGD(model.parameters())`	Defines optimizer for parameter updates.
4	Train Model	`for epoch in range(epochs):`	Implements the training loop.
5	Evaluate Model	`model.eval()`	Evaluates model performance on test data.

Syntax Explanation:

1. Load Dataset

What is Loading a Dataset?
Loading a dataset involves retrieving image data and applying transformations to prepare it for training or evaluation.
Syntax:
```
from torchvision import datasets, transforms

data_transforms = transforms.Compose([
    transforms.Resize((224, 224)),
    transforms.ToTensor(),
    transforms.Normalize(mean=[0.5, 0.5, 0.5],
std=[0.5, 0.5, 0.5])
])

dataset = datasets.ImageFolder(root="data/train",
transform=data_transforms)
```

Detailed Explanation:

- **Purpose:** Loads image data organized in a folder structure (e.g., class-specific subfolders).
- **Parameters:**
    - root: Path to the dataset directory.
    - transform: Transformation pipeline for preprocessing images.
- **Behavior:**
    - Reads images and their corresponding class labels.
    - Prepares data for model input by resizing, normalizing, and converting to tensors.
- **Output:** A dataset object ready for batch loading and training.

Example:

```
train_data = datasets.ImageFolder(root="data/train",
transform=data_transforms)
print(f"Number of classes: {len(train_data.classes)}")
```

Example Explanation:

- Loads training data from the specified directory.
- Displays the number of unique classes in the dataset.

2. Define Model

What is Defining a Model?

Defining a model involves specifying the layers and architecture for image classification.

Syntax:

```
import torch.nn as nn

model = nn.Sequential(
    nn.Conv2d(3, 32, kernel_size=3, stride=1,
padding=1),
    nn.ReLU(),
    nn.MaxPool2d(kernel_size=2, stride=2),
    nn.Flatten(),
    nn.Linear(32 * 112 * 112, 128),
    nn.ReLU(),
    nn.Linear(128, num_classes)
)
```

Detailed Explanation:

- **Purpose:** Defines the architecture of the neural network for the classification task.
- **Components:**
    - `nn.Conv2d`: Convolutional layer for feature extraction.
    - `nn.ReLU`: Activation function for non-linearity.
    - `nn.MaxPool2d`: Pooling layer for dimensionality reduction.
    - `nn.Linear`: Fully connected layer for classification.
    - `nn.Flatten`: Converts feature maps to a 1D vector for the fully connected layers.
- **Behavior:**
    - Processes images through convolutional, pooling, and dense layers.
    - Outputs class probabilities or logits based on the task.
- **Output:** A PyTorch model ready for training.

Example:

```
print(model)
```

Example Explanation:

- Prints the architecture of the defined model.
- Ensures all layers are correctly configured.

3. Compile Training Components

What is Compiling Training Components?

Compiling training components involves setting up the loss function, optimizer, and other configurations needed for model training.

Syntax:

```
import torch.optim as optim

criterion = nn.CrossEntropyLoss()
optimizer = optim.SGD(model.parameters(), lr=0.01,
momentum=0.9)
```

Detailed Explanation:

- **Purpose:** Prepares components to optimize model parameters during training.

- **Components:**
  - criterion: Loss function to compute the error (e.g., CrossEntropyLoss for classification).
  - optimizer: Algorithm to adjust model parameters (e.g., SGD or Adam).
- **Behavior:**
  - Loss function guides the model toward minimizing error.
  - Optimizer updates parameters based on gradients.
- **Output:** Training components ready to be used in the training loop.

Example:

```
print(optimizer)
```

Example Explanation:
- Displays the configuration of the optimizer.
- Confirms learning rate and momentum settings.

4. Train Model

What is Training a Model?

Training a model involves updating its parameters using the training data to minimize the loss function.

Syntax:

```
for epoch in range(epochs):
    model.train()
    for inputs, labels in data_loader:
        inputs, labels = inputs.to(device),
labels.to(device)

        optimizer.zero_grad()
        outputs = model(inputs)
        loss = criterion(outputs, labels)
        loss.backward()
        optimizer.step()
```

Detailed Explanation:
- **Purpose:** Iteratively trains the model to improve its predictions.

- **Steps:**
  - Set the model to training mode with `model.train()`.
  - Iterate over batches of data from the data loader.
  - Compute predictions and calculate the loss.
  - Backpropagate the loss to compute gradients.
  - Update model parameters using the optimizer.
- **Output:** A trained model ready for evaluation.

Example:

```
print(f"Epoch {epoch+1}, Loss: {loss.item():.4f}")
```

Example Explanation:
- Logs the loss for each epoch to monitor training progress.

5. Evaluate Model

What is Evaluating a Model?

Evaluating a model measures its performance on a test dataset to assess accuracy and generalization.

Syntax:

```
model.eval()
with torch.no_grad():
    for inputs, labels in test_loader:
        inputs, labels = inputs.to(device),
labels.to(device)
        outputs = model(inputs)
        _, preds = torch.max(outputs, 1)
        # Compute accuracy
```

Detailed Explanation:
- **Purpose:** Disables gradient computation for efficient evaluation.
- **Steps:**
  - Set the model to evaluation mode with `model.eval()`.
  - Disable gradient tracking using `torch.no_grad()`.
  - Compute predictions and evaluate accuracy.
- **Output:** Model performance metrics, such as accuracy or F1 score.

Example:

```
print(f"Test Accuracy: {accuracy:.2f}%")
```

Example Explanation:
- Logs the test accuracy to assess model generalization.

Real-Life Project:

Project Name: Custom CNN for Image Classification

Project Goal: Build and train a convolutional neural network (CNN) to classify images from a custom dataset.

Code for This Project:

```python
import torch
import torch.nn as nn
import torch.optim as optim
from torchvision import datasets, transforms
from torch.utils.data import DataLoader


# Data preparation
transform = transforms.Compose([
    transforms.Resize((224, 224)),
    transforms.ToTensor(),
    transforms.Normalize(mean=[0.5, 0.5, 0.5],
std=[0.5, 0.5, 0.5])
])

data = datasets.ImageFolder(root="data/train",
transform=transform)
data_loader = DataLoader(data, batch_size=32,
shuffle=True)
# Model definition
model = nn.Sequential(
    nn.Conv2d(3, 32, kernel_size=3, stride=1,
padding=1),
    nn.ReLU(),
    nn.MaxPool2d(kernel_size=2, stride=2),
    nn.Flatten(),
    nn.Linear(32 * 112 * 112, 128),
    nn.ReLU(),
    nn.Linear(128, len(data.classes))
)

# Training components
```

```python
criterion = nn.CrossEntropyLoss()
optimizer = optim.Adam(model.parameters(), lr=0.001)

# Training loop
for epoch in range(10):
    model.train()
    for inputs, labels in data_loader:
        inputs, labels = inputs.to("cuda"),
labels.to("cuda")

        optimizer.zero_grad()
        outputs = model(inputs)
        loss = criterion(outputs, labels)
        loss.backward()
        optimizer.step()

    print(f"Epoch {epoch+1}, Loss: {loss.item():.4f}")

print("Training complete.")
```

Expected Output:

- Training loss decreases over epochs.
- Model becomes capable of classifying images from the custom dataset.

Chapter - 28 Object Detection with PyTorch

Object detection is a computer vision task that involves identifying and localizing objects within an image. PyTorch provides robust tools for implementing object detection models, including pre-trained models in the `torchvision` library and utilities for managing datasets and annotations. This chapter explores how to build, train, and evaluate object detection models using PyTorch.

Key Characteristics of Object Detection Models:
- **Localization and Classification:** Predict both the class and bounding box for each object.
- **Pre-trained Models:** Access to state-of-the-art models like Faster R-CNN, SSD, and RetinaNet.
- **Customizability:** Allows users to fine-tune pre-trained models or build custom architectures.
- **Dataset Support:** Handles popular datasets like COCO, VOC, and custom datasets with ease.
- **Integration:** Seamlessly integrates with PyTorch's training and evaluation workflows.

Steps to Build an Object Detection Model:
1. **Prepare the Dataset:** Load images and annotations in a compatible format.
2. **Choose a Pre-trained Model:** Select a model from `torchvision.models.detection` or define a custom model.
3. **Define Training Components:** Specify the optimizer, learning rate, and loss function.
4. **Train the Model:** Train the model on the dataset while monitoring performance metrics.
5. **Evaluate the Model:** Test the model on unseen data and calculate metrics like mAP (mean Average Precision).
6. **Fine-Tune and Save:** Fine-tune the model if needed and save it for deployment

Syntax Table:

SL No	Function	Syntax/Example	Description
1	Load Dataset	`datasets.CocoDetect ion(root, annFile, transform)`	Loads image data with COCO-style annotations.
2	Load Pre-trained Model	`models.detection.fa sterrcnn_resnet50_f pn(pretrained=True)`	Loads a Faster R-CNN model pre-trained on COCO.
3	Define Optimizer	`torch.optim.SGD(mod el.parameters(), lr=0.005)`	Configures the optimizer for training.
4	Train Model	`model.train()`	Switches the model to training mode.
5	Evaluate Model	`model.eval()`	Switches the model to evaluation mode.

Syntax Explanation:

1. Load Dataset

What is Loading a Dataset?

Loading a dataset involves retrieving images and their corresponding annotations for training or evaluation.

Syntax:

```
from torchvision import datasets, transforms

transform = transforms.Compose([
    transforms.ToTensor()
])

dataset = datasets.CocoDetection(root="data/images",
annFile="data/annotations.json", transform=transform)
```

Detailed Explanation:

- **Purpose:** Loads images and their annotations in the COCO format.

- **Parameters:**
  - ○ root: Directory containing image files.
  - ○ annFile: Path to the JSON file with annotations.
  - ○ transform: Preprocessing steps for the images (e.g., resizing, normalization).
- **Behavior:**
  - ○ Maps each image to its corresponding annotations.
  - ○ Prepares data for training or evaluation.
- **Output:** A dataset object compatible with PyTorch's DataLoader.

Example:

```
print(f"Number of images: {len(dataset)}")
```

Example Explanation:
- Displays the total number of images in the dataset.
- Confirms successful loading of the dataset.

2. Load Pre-trained Model

What is Loading a Pre-trained Model?

Loading a pre-trained object detection model provides a starting point for fine-tuning or inference.

Syntax:

```
from torchvision import models

model = models.detection.fasterrcnn_resnet50_fpn(pretrained=True)
```

Detailed Explanation:
- **Purpose:** Reduces training time by leveraging models pre-trained on large datasets like COCO.
- **Parameters:**
  - ○ pretrained: If True, loads pre-trained weights.
- **Behavior:**
  - ○ Initializes the model with pre-trained weights.
  - ○ Allows fine-tuning by modifying the output layer for custom datasets.
- **Output:** A Faster R-CNN model ready for training or inference.

Example:

```
print(model)
```

Example Explanation:

- Prints the architecture of the pre-trained model.
- Provides an overview of its layers and structure.

3. Define Optimizer

What is Defining an Optimizer?

Defining an optimizer involves specifying the algorithm for updating model parameters during training.

Syntax:

```
import torch.optim as optim

optimizer = optim.SGD(model.parameters(), lr=0.005,
momentum=0.9, weight_decay=0.0005)
```

Detailed Explanation:

- **Purpose:** Configures the optimization algorithm for parameter updates.
- **Parameters:**
  - `model.parameters()`: Model parameters to optimize.
  - `lr`: Learning rate for gradient updates.
  - `momentum`: Factor to accelerate gradient descent.
  - `weight_decay`: Regularization term to prevent overfitting.
- **Behavior:**
  - Adjusts model weights to minimize the loss function.
- **Output:** An optimizer object ready for use in the training loop.

Example:

```
print(optimizer)
```

Example Explanation:

- Displays the optimizer configuration.
- Confirms the learning rate and regularization settings.

4. Train Model

What is Training a Model?
Training a model involves updating its parameters using the training dataset to improve its predictions.
Syntax:

```
model.train()
for images, targets in data_loader:
    images = [img.to(device) for img in images]
    targets = [{k: v.to(device) for k, v in t.items()}
for t in targets]

    optimizer.zero_grad()
    loss_dict = model(images, targets)
    losses = sum(loss for loss in loss_dict.values())
    losses.backward()
    optimizer.step()
```

Detailed Explanation:
- **Purpose:** Optimizes the model to minimize loss.
- **Steps:**
    - Set the model to training mode with `model.train()`.
    - Process batches of images and targets.
    - Compute losses for classification and bounding box regression.
    - Backpropagate the loss and update parameters.
- **Output:** A trained object detection model.

Example:

```
print(f"Loss: {losses.item():.4f}")
```

Example Explanation:
- Logs the total loss for each batch to monitor training progress.

5. Evaluate Model

What is Evaluating a Model?
Evaluating a model involves testing its performance on unseen data and calculating metrics like mAP.

Syntax:

```
model.eval()
with torch.no_grad():
    for images, targets in test_loader:
        images = [img.to(device) for img in images]
        outputs = model(images)
        # Process outputs for evaluation
```

Detailed Explanation:

- **Purpose:** Measures the model's ability to detect objects accurately.
- **Steps:**
  - Set the model to evaluation mode with `model.eval()`.
  - Disable gradient computation using `torch.no_grad()`.
  - Process images and generate predictions.
- **Output:** Metrics such as mAP or precision-recall curves.

Example:

```
print(outputs)
```

Example Explanation:

- Displays the model's predictions, including bounding boxes and class scores.

Real-Life Project:

Project Name: Object Detection with Faster R-CNN

Project Goal: Train and evaluate a Faster R-CNN model on a custom object detection dataset.

Code for This Project:

```
import torch
import torch.optim as optim
from torchvision import datasets, transforms, models
from torch.utils.data import DataLoader

# Data preparation
transform = transforms.Compose([
    transforms.ToTensor()
])

dataset = datasets.CocoDetection(root="data/images",
annFile="data/annotations.json", transform=transform)
```

```python
data_loader = DataLoader(dataset, batch_size=4,
shuffle=True)

# Load pre-trained model
model =
models.detection.fasterrcnn_resnet50_fpn(pretrained=Tru
e)
model.to("cuda")

# Define optimizer
optimizer = optim.SGD(model.parameters(), lr=0.005,
momentum=0.9, weight_decay=0.0005)

# Training loop
for epoch in range(10):
    model.train()
    for images, targets in data_loader:
        images = [img.to("cuda") for img in images]
        targets = [{k: v.to("cuda") for k, v in
t.items()} for t in targets]

        optimizer.zero_grad()
        loss_dict = model(images, targets)
        losses = sum(loss for loss in
loss_dict.values())
        losses.backward()
        optimizer.step()

    print(f"Epoch {epoch+1}, Loss:
{losses.item():.4f}")

print("Training complete.")
```

Expected Output:
- Logs training loss for each epoch.
- Outputs a trained object detection model ready for evaluation or deployment.

Chapter - 29 Semantic and Instance Segmentation

Semantic and instance segmentation are advanced computer vision tasks that involve partitioning an image into meaningful segments. Semantic segmentation assigns a label to every pixel in the image, while instance segmentation differentiates between individual objects within the same class. PyTorch, along with its `torchvision` library, provides pre-trained models, utilities, and APIs to implement both tasks efficiently. This chapter covers the fundamental concepts and step-by-step implementation of semantic and instance segmentation using PyTorch.

Key Characteristics of Segmentation Tasks:
- **Semantic Segmentation:** Labels every pixel in the image with a class (e.g., sky, car, road).
- **Instance Segmentation:** Differentiates between individual instances of the same object class.
- **Pre-trained Models:** Includes state-of-the-art models like DeepLabV3 and Mask R-CNN.
- **Customizability:** Supports fine-tuning for custom datasets.
- **Dataset Compatibility:** Works with standard datasets like COCO, Pascal VOC, and Cityscapes.

Steps to Implement Segmentation Models:
1. **Prepare the Dataset:** Load and preprocess the dataset with annotations.
2. **Choose a Pre-trained Model:** Select a model like DeepLabV3 for semantic segmentation or Mask R-CNN for instance segmentation.
3. **Define Training Components:** Configure the optimizer, loss function, and training loop.
4. **Train the Model:** Train the model on the dataset and monitor loss and metrics.
5. **Evaluate the Model:** Test the model on unseen data and calculate metrics like IoU (Intersection over Union).
6. **Fine-Tune and Save:** Fine-tune the model and save it for deployment.

Syntax Table:

SL No	Function	Syntax/Example	Description
1	Load Dataset	`datasets.CocoDetec tion(root, annFile, transform)`	Loads dataset with COCO-style annotations.
2	Load Pre-trained Model	`models.segmentatio n.deeplabv3_resnet 50(pretrained=True )`	Loads DeepLabV3 pre-trained on COCO.
3	Define Optimizer	`torch.optim.Adam(m odel.parameters(), lr=0.001)`	Configures the optimizer for training.
4	Train Model	`model.train()`	Switches the model to training mode.
5	Evaluate Model	`model.eval()`	Switches the model to evaluation mode.

Syntax Explanation:

1. Load Dataset

What is Loading a Dataset?
Loading a dataset involves retrieving images and their corresponding segmentation masks for training or evaluation.
Syntax:
```
from torchvision import datasets, transforms

transform = transforms.Compose([
    transforms.ToTensor()
])

dataset = datasets.CocoDetection(root="data/images",
annFile="data/annotations.json", transform=transform)
```

Detailed Explanation:
- **Purpose:** Loads image and mask pairs from a dataset.
- **Parameters:**
  - `root`: Directory containing the images.
  - `annFile`: Path to the annotation file (e.g., COCO format).
  - `transform`: Transformation pipeline for image preprocessing.
- **Behavior:**
  - Maps each image to its corresponding segmentation mask.
  - Applies transformations like resizing or normalization.
- **Output:** A dataset object ready for training or evaluation.

Example:
```
print(f"Number of images: {len(dataset)}")
```

Example Explanation:
- Displays the number of image-mask pairs in the dataset.
- Confirms successful dataset loading.

2. Load Pre-trained Model

What is Loading a Pre-trained Model?
Loading a pre-trained model provides a starting point for segmentation tasks, allowing fine-tuning or direct inference.

Syntax:
```
from torchvision import models
model =
models.segmentation.deeplabv3_resnet50(pretrained=True)
```

Detailed Explanation:
- **Purpose:** Reduces training time by using models pre-trained on large datasets like COCO.
- **Parameters:**
  - `pretrained`: If True, loads pre-trained weights.
- **Behavior:**
  - Initializes the model with pre-trained weights.

      o   Outputs segmentation masks with class probabilities.
- **Output:** A segmentation model ready for training or inference.

Example:
```
print(model)
```

Example Explanation:
- Displays the architecture of the pre-trained model.
- Shows the input and output configurations.

3. Define Optimizer

What is Defining an Optimizer?
Defining an optimizer specifies the algorithm to update model parameters during training.
Syntax:
```
import torch.optim as optim

optimizer = optim.Adam(model.parameters(), lr=0.001)
```
Detailed Explanation:
- **Purpose:** Optimizes the model's weights to minimize the loss function.
- **Parameters:**
  - o   `model.parameters()`: Parameters to optimize.
  - o   `lr`: Learning rate for updates.
- **Behavior:**
  - o   Updates weights based on gradients calculated during backpropagation.
- **Output:** An optimizer object ready for use in the training loop.

Example:
```
print(optimizer)
```
Example Explanation:
- Displays the optimizer configuration.
- Confirms the learning rate and parameters being optimized.

4. Train Model

What is Training a Model?

Training a model involves updating its parameters using training data to improve segmentation accuracy.

Syntax:

```
model.train()
for images, targets in data_loader:
    images = [img.to(device) for img in images]
    targets = [t.to(device) for t in targets]

    optimizer.zero_grad()
    outputs = model(images)
    loss = criterion(outputs, targets)
    loss.backward()
    optimizer.step()
```

Detailed Explanation:

- **Purpose:** Optimizes the model to improve segmentation performance.
- **Steps:**
  - Set the model to training mode with `model.train()`.
  - Load image-mask pairs in batches from the data loader.
  - Compute the loss between predictions and ground truth.
  - Backpropagate the loss and update weights using the optimizer.
- **Output:** A trained segmentation model.

Example:

```
print(f"Loss: {loss.item():.4f}")
```

Example Explanation:

- Logs the loss for each batch to monitor training progress.

5. Evaluate Model

What is Evaluating a Model?

Evaluating a model involves testing its performance on unseen data to measure metrics like IoU.

Syntax:

```
model.eval()
with torch.no_grad():
    for images, targets in test_loader:
        images = [img.to(device) for img in images]
        outputs = model(images)
        # Process outputs to compute metrics
```

Detailed Explanation:

- **Purpose:** Measures the model's ability to segment images accurately.
- **Steps:**
  - o Set the model to evaluation mode with `model.eval()`.
  - o Disable gradient computation using `torch.no_grad()`.
  - o Process test images to generate predictions.
- **Output:** Segmentation metrics such as IoU or pixel-wise accuracy.

Example:

```
print(outputs)
```

Example Explanation:

- Displays predicted segmentation masks.
- Confirms the model's ability to generate meaningful predictions.

Real-Life Project:

Project Name: Semantic Segmentation with DeepLabV3

Project Goal: Train and evaluate a DeepLabV3 model on a custom semantic segmentation dataset.

Code for This Project:

```
import torch
import torch.optim as optim
from torchvision import datasets, transforms, models
from torch.utils.data import DataLoader

# Data preparation
transform = transforms.Compose([
    transforms.ToTensor()
])
```

```python
dataset = datasets.CocoDetection(root="data/images",
annFile="data/annotations.json", transform=transform)
data_loader = DataLoader(dataset, batch_size=4,
shuffle=True)

# Load pre-trained model
model =
models.segmentation.deeplabv3_resnet50(pretrained=True)
model.to("cuda")

# Define optimizer
optimizer = optim.Adam(model.parameters(), lr=0.001)

# Training loop
for epoch in range(10):
    model.train()
    for images, targets in data_loader:
        images = [img.to("cuda") for img in images]
        targets = [t.to("cuda") for t in targets]

        optimizer.zero_grad()
        outputs = model(images)
        loss = criterion(outputs["out"], targets)
        loss.backward()
        optimizer.step()

    print(f"Epoch {epoch+1}, Loss: {loss.item():.4f}")

print("Training complete.")
```

Expected Output:

- Logs training loss for each epoch.
- Outputs a trained segmentation model ready for evaluation or deployment.

Chapter - 30 Image Generation with GANs in PyTorch

Generative Adversarial Networks (GANs) are a class of neural networks used for generating realistic images and other data types. A GAN consists of two components: a generator that creates synthetic data and a discriminator that evaluates its authenticity. PyTorch provides powerful tools to implement, train, and evaluate GANs. This chapter explores the process of building and training GANs for image generation tasks.

Key Characteristics of GANs:
- **Generator and Discriminator:** Two neural networks that compete in a minimax game.
- **Adversarial Training:** The generator aims to fool the discriminator, while the discriminator strives to distinguish real from fake data.
- **Applications:** Image generation, style transfer, data augmentation, and more.
- **Customizability:** Users can design custom architectures and loss functions.
- **Stability Challenges:** Training GANs can be unstable and requires careful tuning.

Steps to Build a GAN:
1. **Design the Generator:** Define a neural network to generate synthetic images from random noise.
2. **Design the Discriminator:** Create a neural network to classify images as real or fake.
3. **Define Loss Functions:** Use adversarial loss for both generator and discriminator.
4. **Set Up Training Pipeline:** Train the generator and discriminator alternately.
5. **Evaluate Results:** Monitor generated images and loss values.

Syntax Table:

SL No	Function	Syntax/Example	Description
1	Define Generator	`nn.Sequential (*layers)`	Constructs the generator network.
2	Define Discriminator	`nn.Sequential (*layers)`	Constructs the discriminator network.
3	Initialize Optimizers	`torch.optim.A dam(params, lr=lr)`	Configures optimizers for training.
4	Compute Loss	`criterion(out put, target)`	Computes adversarial loss for training.
5	Generate Images	`generator(noi se)`	Produces synthetic images from random noise.

Syntax Explanation:

1. Define Generator

What is a Generator?
The generator is a neural network that takes random noise as input and produces synthetic images as output.
Syntax:
```
import torch.nn as nn

generator = nn.Sequential(
    nn.Linear(100, 256),
    nn.ReLU(),
    nn.Linear(256, 512),
    nn.ReLU(),
    nn.Linear(512, 1024),
    nn.ReLU(),
    nn.Linear(1024, 784),
    nn.Tanh()
)
```
Detailed Explanation:

- **Purpose:** Converts random noise into an image-like structure by mapping a low-dimensional vector to high-dimensional image space.
- **Components:**
  - **nn.Linear:** Fully connected layers expand and transform the input vector.
  - **nn.ReLU:** Introduces non-linearity to enable the generator to model complex patterns.
  - **nn.Tanh:** Normalizes output values to [-1, 1], suitable for images.
- **Process:**
  - Takes a random vector (e.g., of size 100).
  - Sequentially transforms it into an image vector of size 784 (28x28 for MNIST).
  - Outputs synthetic images normalized for training.
- **Output:** A PyTorch sequential model for the generator.

Example:
```
print(generator)
```
Example Explanation:
- Confirms the layer structure and flow within the generator.
- Ensures all transformations align with input and output dimensions.

2. Define Discriminator

What is a Discriminator?
The discriminator is a neural network that evaluates whether input images are real or generated by the generator.
Syntax:
```
import torch.nn as nn

discriminator = nn.Sequential(
    nn.Linear(784, 512),
    nn.LeakyReLU(0.2),
    nn.Linear(512, 256),
```

```
    nn.LeakyReLU(0.2),
    nn.Linear(256, 1),
    nn.Sigmoid()
)
```

Detailed Explanation:

- **Purpose:** Classifies input images as real or fake.
- **Components:**
  - **nn.Linear:** Fully connected layers reduce the dimensionality of the input.
  - **nn.LeakyReLU:** Introduces slight gradients for negative inputs to prevent dead neurons.
  - **nn.Sigmoid:** Outputs probabilities (values between 0 and 1).
- **Process:**
  - Takes a flattened image vector (e.g., 784 pixels for MNIST).
  - Processes through layers, reducing to a single scalar probability.
  - Returns the likelihood of the input being real.
- **Output:** A PyTorch sequential model for the discriminator.

Example:
```
print(discriminator)
```
Example Explanation:

- Displays the layers in the discriminator.
- Verifies that the output is a scalar (single probability).

3. Initialize Optimizers

What are Optimizers?

Optimizers adjust the model parameters based on the gradients to minimize loss functions during training.

Syntax:
```
import torch.optim as optim
optimizer_g = optim.Adam(generator.parameters(),
lr=0.0002)
optimizer_d = optim.Adam(discriminator.parameters(),
lr=0.0002)
```

Detailed Explanation:

- **Purpose:** Configures optimization strategies for training the generator and discriminator.
- **Parameters:**
  - `parameters()`: Specifies which model parameters to update.
  - `lr`: Sets the learning rate for gradient updates.
- **Process:**
  - `optimizer_g`: Updates the generator to produce images that better fool the discriminator.
  - `optimizer_d`: Updates the discriminator to improve its ability to distinguish real from fake images.
- **Output:** Separate optimizers for both networks.

Example:
```
print(optimizer_g)
```
Example Explanation:

- Displays details about the generator's optimizer, such as learning rate and parameter count.

4. Compute Loss

What is Adversarial Loss?

Adversarial loss evaluates the performance of the generator and discriminator based on their ability to fool or identify.

Syntax:
```
criterion = nn.BCELoss()

# For real images
loss_real = criterion(discriminator(real_images),
torch.ones(batch_size, 1))

# For fake images
loss_fake = criterion(discriminator(fake_images),
torch.zeros(batch_size, 1))
```

Detailed Explanation:

- **Purpose:** Measures the binary cross-entropy loss for real and fake predictions.
- **Parameters:**
  - **output:** The discriminator's prediction.
  - **target:** The true label (1 for real, 0 for fake).
- **Process:**
  - Computes `loss_real` by comparing discriminator predictions on real images with a tensor of ones.
  - Computes `loss_fake` by comparing predictions on fake images with a tensor of zeros.
  - Guides the generator to improve fake image quality and the discriminator to refine its classification.
- **Output:** Loss values for real and fake predictions.

Example:

```
print(f"Loss Real: {loss_real.item():.4f}, Loss Fake:
{loss_fake.item():.4f}")
```

Example Explanation:

- Logs individual loss contributions for real and fake images, aiding debugging.

5. Generate Images

What is Generating Images?
Generating images uses the generator to create synthetic images from random noise inputs.
Syntax:
```
noise = torch.randn(batch_size, 100)
synthetic_images = generator(noise)
```
Detailed Explanation:

- **Purpose:** Produces synthetic images using the trained generator.
- **Steps:**
  - Sample random noise from a standard normal distribution.

- o Pass the noise through the generator network.
- **Process:**
  - o Generates a batch of images normalized to [-1, 1].
  - o Converts noise into meaningful data structures that resemble real images.
- **Output:** A batch of generated images ready for visualization or evaluation.

Example:
```
print(synthetic_images.shape)
```
Example Explanation:
- Confirms the dimensions of the generated images, ensuring correctness in batch size and resolution.

Real-Life Project:
Project Name: Handwritten Digit Generation with GANs
Project Goal: Train a GAN to generate realistic handwritten digits similar to those in the MNIST dataset.

Code for This Project:

```python
import torch
import torch.nn as nn
import torch.optim as optim
from torchvision import datasets, transforms
from torch.utils.data import DataLoader

# Data preparation
transform = transforms.Compose([
    transforms.ToTensor(),
    transforms.Normalize((0.5,), (0.5,))
])

dataset = datasets.MNIST(root="data", train=True,
download=True, transform=transform)
data_loader = DataLoader(dataset, batch_size=64,
shuffle=True)
```

```python
# Define generator and discriminator
generator = nn.Sequential(
    nn.Linear(100, 256),
    nn.ReLU(),
    nn.Linear(256, 512),
    nn.ReLU(),
    nn.Linear(512, 1024),
    nn.ReLU(),
    nn.Linear(1024, 784),
    nn.Tanh()
)

discriminator = nn.Sequential(
    nn.Linear(784, 512),
    nn.LeakyReLU(0.2),
    nn.Linear(512, 256),
    nn.LeakyReLU(0.2),
    nn.Linear(256, 1),
    nn.Sigmoid()
)

# Initialize optimizers
optimizer_g = optim.Adam(generator.parameters(),
lr=0.0002)
optimizer_d = optim.Adam(discriminator.parameters(),
lr=0.0002)

# Loss function
criterion = nn.BCELoss()

# Training loop
for epoch in range(50):
    for real_images, _ in data_loader:
        batch_size = real_images.size(0)
        real_images = real_images.view(batch_size, -1)
```

```python
        # Train discriminator
        optimizer_d.zero_grad()
        noise = torch.randn(batch_size, 100)
        fake_images = generator(noise)

        loss_real =
criterion(discriminator(real_images),
torch.ones(batch_size, 1))
        loss_fake =
criterion(discriminator(fake_images),
torch.zeros(batch_size, 1))
        loss_d = loss_real + loss_fake
        loss_d.backward()
        optimizer_d.step()

        # Train generator
        optimizer_g.zero_grad()
        fake_images = generator(noise)
        loss_g = criterion(discriminator(fake_images),
torch.ones(batch_size, 1))
        loss_g.backward()
        optimizer_g.step()

    print(f"Epoch {epoch+1}, Loss D:
{loss_d.item():.4f}, Loss G: {loss_g.item():.4f}")

print("Training complete.")
```

Expected Output:

- Logs training loss for the generator and discriminator for each epoch.
- Outputs realistic handwritten digits after training.

Chapter - 31 Image Generation with GANs in PyTorch

Generative Adversarial Networks (GANs) are a class of neural networks used for generating realistic images and other data types. A GAN consists of two components: a generator that creates synthetic data and a discriminator that evaluates its authenticity. PyTorch provides powerful tools to implement, train, and evaluate GANs. This chapter explores the process of building and training GANs for image generation tasks.

Key Characteristics of GANs:

- **Generator and Discriminator:** Two neural networks that compete in a minimax game.
- **Adversarial Training:** The generator aims to fool the discriminator, while the discriminator strives to distinguish real from fake data.
- **Applications:** Image generation, style transfer, data augmentation, and more.
- **Customizability:** Users can design custom architectures and loss functions.
- **Stability Challenges:** Training GANs can be unstable and requires careful tuning.

Steps to Build a GAN:

1. **Design the Generator:** Define a neural network to generate synthetic images from random noise.
2. **Design the Discriminator:** Create a neural network to classify images as real or fake.
3. **Define Loss Functions:** Use adversarial loss for both generator and discriminator.
4. **Set Up Training Pipeline:** Train the generator and discriminator alternately.
5. **Evaluate Results:** Monitor generated images and loss values.

Syntax Table:

SL No	Function	Syntax/Example	Description
1	Define Generator	`nn.Sequential(* layers)`	Constructs the generator network.
2	Define Discriminator	`nn.Sequential(* layers)`	Constructs the discriminator network.
3	Initialize Optimizers	`torch.optim.Ada m(params, lr=lr)`	Configures optimizers for training.
4	Compute Loss	`criterion(outpu t, target)`	Computes adversarial loss for training.
5	Generate Images	`generator(noise )`	Produces synthetic images from random noise.

Syntax Explanation:

1. Define Generator

What is a Generator?
The generator is a neural network that takes random noise as input and produces synthetic images as output.

Syntax:

```
import torch.nn as nn
generator = nn.Sequential(
    nn.Linear(100, 256),
    nn.ReLU(),
    nn.Linear(256, 512),
    nn.ReLU(),
    nn.Linear(512, 1024),
    nn.ReLU(),
    nn.Linear(1024, 784),
    nn.Tanh()
)
```

Detailed Explanation:

- **Purpose:** Converts random noise into an image-like structure by mapping a low-dimensional vector to high-dimensional image space.
- **Components:**
    - **nn.Linear:** Fully connected layers expand and transform the input vector.
    - **nn.ReLU:** Introduces non-linearity to enable the generator to model complex patterns.
    - **nn.Tanh:** Normalizes output values to [-1, 1], suitable for images.
- **Process:**
    - Takes a random vector (e.g., of size 100).
    - Sequentially transforms it into an image vector of size 784 (28x28 for MNIST).
    - Outputs synthetic images normalized for training.
- **Output:** A PyTorch sequential model for the generator.

Example:

```
print(generator)
```

Example Explanation:

- Confirms the layer structure and flow within the generator.
- Ensures all transformations align with input and output dimensions.

2. Define Discriminator

What is a Discriminator?

The discriminator is a neural network that evaluates whether input images are real or generated by the generator.

Syntax:

```
import torch.nn as nn

discriminator = nn.Sequential(
    nn.Linear(784, 512),
    nn.LeakyReLU(0.2),
    nn.Linear(512, 256),
```

```
    nn.LeakyReLU(0.2),
    nn.Linear(256, 1),
    nn.Sigmoid()
)
```

Detailed Explanation:

- **Purpose:** Classifies input images as real or fake.
- **Components:**
  - **nn.Linear:** Fully connected layers reduce the dimensionality of the input.
  - **nn.LeakyReLU:** Introduces slight gradients for negative inputs to prevent dead neurons.
  - **nn.Sigmoid:** Outputs probabilities (values between 0 and 1).
- **Process:**
  - Takes a flattened image vector (e.g., 784 pixels for MNIST).
  - Processes through layers, reducing to a single scalar probability.
  - Returns the likelihood of the input being real.
- **Output:** A PyTorch sequential model for the discriminator.

Example:
```
print(discriminator)
```
Example Explanation:

- Displays the layers in the discriminator.
- Verifies that the output is a scalar (single probability).

3. Initialize Optimizers

What are Optimizers?

Optimizers adjust the model parameters based on the gradients to minimize loss functions during training.

Syntax:
```
import torch.optim as optim

optimizer_g = optim.Adam(generator.parameters(),
lr=0.0002)
optimizer_d = optim.Adam(discriminator.parameters(),
lr=0.0002)
```

Detailed Explanation:

- **Purpose:** Configures optimization strategies for training the generator and discriminator.
- **Parameters:**
    - `parameters()`: Specifies which model parameters to update.
    - `lr`: Sets the learning rate for gradient updates.
- **Process:**
    - `optimizer_g`: Updates the generator to produce images that better fool the discriminator.
    - `optimizer_d`: Updates the discriminator to improve its ability to distinguish real from fake images.
- **Output:** Separate optimizers for both networks.

Example:

```
print(optimizer_g)
```

Example Explanation:

- Displays details about the generator's optimizer, such as learning rate and parameter count.

4. Compute Loss

What is Adversarial Loss?

Adversarial loss evaluates the performance of the generator and discriminator based on their ability to fool or identify.

Syntax:

```
criterion = nn.BCELoss()

# For real images
loss_real = criterion(discriminator(real_images),
torch.ones(batch_size, 1))

# For fake images
loss_fake = criterion(discriminator(fake_images),
torch.zeros(batch_size, 1))
```

Detailed Explanation:

- **Purpose:** Measures the binary cross-entropy loss for real and fake predictions.
- **Parameters:**
  - `output`: The discriminator's prediction.
  - `target`: The true label (1 for real, 0 for fake).
- **Process:**
  - Computes `loss_real` by comparing discriminator predictions on real images with a tensor of ones.
  - Computes `loss_fake` by comparing predictions on fake images with a tensor of zeros.
  - Guides the generator to improve fake image quality and the discriminator to refine its classification.
- **Output:** Loss values for real and fake predictions.

Example:

```
print(f"Loss Real: {loss_real.item():.4f}, Loss Fake:
{loss_fake.item():.4f}")
```

Example Explanation:

- Logs individual loss contributions for real and fake images, aiding debugging.

5. Generate Images

What is Generating Images?
Generating images uses the generator to create synthetic images from random noise inputs.

Syntax:
```
noise = torch.randn(batch_size, 100)
synthetic_images = generator(noise)
```

Detailed Explanation:
- **Purpose:** Produces synthetic images using the trained generator.
- **Steps:**

- o Sample random noise from a standard normal distribution.
- o Pass the noise through the generator network.
- **Process:**
  - o Generates a batch of images normalized to [-1, 1].
  - o Converts noise into meaningful data structures that resemble real images.
- **Output:** A batch of generated images ready for visualization or evaluation.

Example:

```
print(synthetic_images.shape)
```

Example Explanation:

- Confirms the dimensions of the generated images, ensuring correctness in batch size and resolution.

Real-Life Project:

Project Name: Handwritten Digit Generation with GANs

Project Goal: Train a GAN to generate realistic handwritten digits similar to those in the MNIST dataset.

Code for This Project:

```
import torch
import torch.nn as nn
import torch.optim as optim
from torchvision import datasets, transforms
from torch.utils.data import DataLoader


# Data preparation
transform = transforms.Compose([
    transforms.ToTensor(),
    transforms.Normalize((0.5,), (0.5,))
])

dataset = datasets.MNIST(root="data", train=True,
download=True, transform=transform)
data_loader = DataLoader(dataset, batch_size=64,
shuffle=True)


# Define generator and discriminator
```

```python
generator = nn.Sequential(
    nn.Linear(100, 256),
    nn.ReLU(),
    nn.Linear(256, 512),
    nn.ReLU(),
    nn.Linear(512, 1024),
    nn.ReLU(),
    nn.Linear(1024, 784),
    nn.Tanh()
)

discriminator = nn.Sequential(
    nn.Linear(784, 512),
    nn.LeakyReLU(0.2),
    nn.Linear(512, 256),
    nn.LeakyReLU(0.2),
    nn.Linear(256, 1),
    nn.Sigmoid()
)

# Initialize optimizers
optimizer_g = optim.Adam(generator.parameters(),
lr=0.0002)
optimizer_d = optim.Adam(discriminator.parameters(),
lr=0.0002)

# Loss function
criterion = nn.BCELoss()

# Training loop
for epoch in range(50):
    for real_images, _ in data_loader:
        batch_size = real_images.size(0)
        real_images = real_images.view(batch_size, -1)

        # Train discriminator
        optimizer_d.zero_grad()
```

```
            noise = torch.randn(batch_size, 100)
            fake_images = generator(noise)

            loss_real =
criterion(discriminator(real_images),
torch.ones(batch_size, 1))
            loss_fake =
criterion(discriminator(fake_images),
torch.zeros(batch_size, 1))
            loss_d = loss_real + loss_fake
            loss_d.backward()
            optimizer_d.step()

            # Train generator
            optimizer_g.zero_grad()
            fake_images = generator(noise)
            loss_g = criterion(discriminator(fake_images),
torch.ones(batch_size, 1))
            loss_g.backward()
            optimizer_g.step()

    print(f"Epoch {epoch+1}, Loss D:
{loss_d.item():.4f}, Loss G: {loss_g.item():.4f}")

print("Training complete.")
```

Expected Output:

- Logs training loss for the generator and discriminator for each epoch.
- Outputs realistic handwritten digits after training.

Chapter – 32 Transfer Learning for Computer Vision Tasks

Transfer learning is a machine learning technique that leverages pre-trained models to solve new tasks with limited data. In computer vision, pre-trained models trained on large datasets, such as ImageNet, serve as excellent starting points for tasks like classification, detection, and segmentation. PyTorch provides robust tools for implementing transfer learning efficiently. This chapter covers how to adapt pre-trained models for custom vision tasks using PyTorch.

Key Characteristics of Transfer Learning:

- **Pre-trained Models:** Utilizes models trained on extensive datasets to transfer knowledge.
- **Fine-Tuning:** Adjusts the pre-trained model's weights for a specific task.
- **Feature Extraction:** Uses the pre-trained model as a fixed feature extractor.
- **Efficiency:** Reduces training time and improves performance on small datasets.
- **Applications:** Image classification, object detection, segmentation, and more.

Steps for Transfer Learning:

1. **Select a Pre-trained Model:** Choose a model from PyTorch's `torchvision.models` library.
2. **Replace the Output Layer:** Modify the final layer to match the number of classes in the custom dataset.
3. **Freeze Layers (Optional):** Freeze earlier layers to retain pre-trained features.
4. **Define Training Components:** Set up the optimizer, loss function, and data loaders.
5. **Train and Fine-Tune:** Train the modified model on the new dataset.
6. **Evaluate and Save:** Test the model and save it for deployment.

Syntax Table:

SL No	Function	Syntax/Example	Description
1	Load Pre-trained Model	`models.resnet18(pre trained=True)`	Loads a pre-trained ResNet-18 model.
2	Modify Output Layer	`model.fc = nn.Linear(in_featur es, num_classes)`	Replaces the final layer for custom tasks.
3	Freeze Layers	`for param in model.parameters(): param.requires_grad = False`	Prevents updates to pre-trained weights.
4	Define Optimizer	`torch.optim.SGD(mod el.parameters(), lr=0.01)`	Configures the optimizer for training.
5	Train Model	`model.train()`	Switches the model to training mode.

Syntax Explanation:

1. Load Pre-trained Model

What is Loading a Pre-trained Model?
Loading a pre-trained model provides a foundation for transfer learning by utilizing models trained on large datasets.

Syntax:
```
from torchvision import models
model = models.resnet18(pretrained=True)
```

Detailed Explanation:
- **Purpose:** Leverages the knowledge of a pre-trained model for a new task.
- **Parameters:**
  - pretrained: If True, loads weights trained on a large dataset like ImageNet.

- **Behavior:**
  - ○ Initializes the model with pre-trained weights.
  - ○ Outputs a model ready for adaptation.
- **Output:** A pre-trained ResNet-18 model.

Example:
```
print(model)
```

Example Explanation:
- Displays the architecture of the ResNet-18 model.
- Confirms the presence of pre-trained weights.

2. Modify Output Layer

What is Modifying the Output Layer?
Replacing the final layer adapts the pre-trained model to match the number of classes in the new dataset.

Syntax:
```
import torch.nn as nn

model.fc = nn.Linear(in_features=model.fc.in_features,
out_features=num_classes)
```

Detailed Explanation:
- **Purpose:** Adjusts the model for the specific number of output classes in the custom task.
- **Parameters:**
  - ○ `in_features`: Number of input features to the output layer.
  - ○ `out_features`: Number of classes in the custom dataset.
- **Behavior:**
  - ○ Replaces the original fully connected layer with a new one.
  - ○ Fine-tunes the new layer during training.
- **Output:** A model tailored for the new classification task.

Example:
```
print(model.fc)
```

Example Explanation:
- Displays the modified fully connected layer.
- Ensures the new output dimensions align with the task requirements.

3. Freeze Layers

What is Freezing Layers?
Freezing layers prevents updates to the weights of earlier layers, retaining pre-trained features.

Syntax:
```
for param in model.parameters():
    param.requires_grad = False
```

Detailed Explanation:
- **Purpose:** Focuses training on specific layers while preserving the knowledge of earlier layers.
- **Process:**
  - Iterates through all model parameters.
  - Sets requires_grad to False for layers to freeze.
- **Behavior:**
  - Prevents gradient updates to frozen layers.
  - Reduces computational overhead and overfitting.
- **Output:** A partially frozen model ready for fine-tuning.

Example:
```
for name, param in model.named_parameters():
    print(f"{name}: {param.requires_grad}")
```

Example Explanation:
- Logs the gradient status of each layer.
- Verifies which layers are frozen and trainable.

4. Define Optimizer

What is Defining an Optimizer?
Optimizers adjust the weights of trainable layers based on the gradients to minimize loss functions.

Syntax:
```
import torch.optim as optim

optimizer = optim.SGD(model.parameters(), lr=0.01,
momentum=0.9)
```
Detailed Explanation:
- **Purpose:** Configures the optimization algorithm for training.
- **Parameters:**
    - `parameters()`: Specifies which model parameters to optimize.
    - `lr`: Sets the learning rate for updates.
    - `momentum`: Adds inertia to gradient updates for smoother convergence.
- **Behavior:**
    - Updates trainable weights to minimize the loss function.
- **Output:** An optimizer ready for use in the training loop.

Example:
```
print(optimizer)
```

Example Explanation:
- Displays the optimizer configuration.
- Confirms learning rate and parameters being optimized.

5. Train Model

What is Training a Model?
Training a model involves iteratively updating its parameters to minimize the loss function.
Syntax:
```
model.train()
for inputs, labels in data_loader:
    inputs, labels = inputs.to(device),
labels.to(device)

    optimizer.zero_grad()
    outputs = model(inputs)
```

```
loss = criterion(outputs, labels)
loss.backward()
optimizer.step()
```

Detailed Explanation:
- **Purpose:** Optimizes the model's weights to improve task performance.
- **Steps:**
  - Sets the model to training mode with `model.train()`.
  - Processes batches of input data.
  - Computes predictions and calculates the loss.
  - Updates weights using the optimizer.
- **Output:** A fine-tuned model ready for evaluation.

Example:
```
print(f"Loss: {loss.item():.4f}")
```

Example Explanation:
- Logs the loss for each batch to monitor training progress.

Real-Life Project:
Project Name: Transfer Learning for Image Classification
Project Goal: Fine-tune a pre-trained ResNet-18 model to classify images from a custom dataset.

Code for This Project:

```
import torch
import torch.nn as nn
import torch.optim as optim
from torchvision import datasets, transforms, models
from torch.utils.data import DataLoader

# Data preparation
transform = transforms.Compose([
    transforms.Resize((224, 224)),
    transforms.ToTensor(),
    transforms.Normalize(mean=[0.5, 0.5, 0.5],
```

```python
                std=[0.5, 0.5, 0.5])
])
dataset = datasets.ImageFolder(root="data/train",
transform=transform)
data_loader = DataLoader(dataset, batch_size=32,
shuffle=True)
# Load pre-trained model
model = models.resnet18(pretrained=True)
model.fc = nn.Linear(model.fc.in_features, num_classes)
# Freeze earlier layers
for param in model.parameters():
    param.requires_grad = False

# Unfreeze the final fully connected layer
for param in model.fc.parameters():
    param.requires_grad = True
# Define optimizer and loss function
optimizer = optim.Adam(model.fc.parameters(), lr=0.001)
criterion = nn.CrossEntropyLoss()
# Training loop
for epoch in range(10):
    model.train()
    for inputs, labels in data_loader:
        inputs, labels = inputs.to("cuda"),
labels.to("cuda")
        optimizer.zero_grad()
        outputs = model(inputs)
        loss = criterion(outputs, labels)
        loss.backward()
        optimizer.step()

    print(f"Epoch {epoch+1}, Loss: {loss.item():.4f}")

print("Training complete.")
```

Expected Output:
- Logs training loss for each epoch.
- Outputs a fine-tuned model ready for evaluation or deployment.

Chapter - 33 Working with Text Data in PyTorch

Text data is a crucial component of natural language processing (NLP) tasks. PyTorch provides various tools to preprocess, represent, and model text data effectively. From tokenization to building embeddings, PyTorch simplifies the workflow with its utilities like `torchtext` and support for custom implementations. This chapter covers the essentials of handling text data in PyTorch, including tokenization, embeddings, and preparing data loaders for NLP models.

Key Characteristics of Text Data Processing:
- **Tokenization:** Converts raw text into tokens for easier processing.
- **Embeddings:** Represents words or tokens in dense vector spaces.
- **Padding and Truncation:** Ensures uniform sequence lengths for batching.
- **Custom Datasets:** Allows creation of text datasets tailored to specific tasks.
- **Integration:** Seamlessly integrates with PyTorch's model and training pipeline.

Steps for Processing Text Data:
1. **Preprocess Text:** Tokenize, clean, and standardize raw text.
2. **Build Vocabulary:** Map tokens to unique numerical identifiers.
3. **Convert Tokens to Tensors:** Prepare numerical data for PyTorch models.
4. **Apply Embeddings:** Represent words or sequences as dense vectors.
5. **Prepare Data Loaders:** Organize text data into batches for training and evaluation.

Syntax Table:

SL No	Function	Syntax/Example	Description
1	Tokenize Text	`tokenizer(text)`	Converts raw text into a list of tokens.
2	Create Vocabulary	`vocab = Vocab(counter, max_size=max_vocab _size)`	Builds a vocabulary from a tokenized dataset.
3	Numericalize Tokens	`[vocab[token] for token in tokens]`	Converts tokens into numerical indices.
4	Apply Embeddings	`embedding = nn.Embedding(num_e mbeddings, embed_dim)`	Maps tokens to dense vectors.
5	Create DataLoader	`DataLoader(dataset , batch_size=batch_s ize)`	Prepares batches of text data for training.

Syntax Explanation:

1. Tokenize Text

What is Tokenization?
Tokenization is the process of breaking raw text into smaller units, such as words, subwords, or characters.

Syntax:
```
from torchtext.data.utils import get_tokenizer
tokenizer = get_tokenizer("basic_english")
tokens = tokenizer("This is a sample text.")
```

Detailed Explanation:
- **Purpose:** Converts unstructured text into structured tokens for further processing.
- **Steps:**
  - Use a tokenizer function (e.g., `basic_english`) to split

text into tokens.

- o Handle punctuation, case normalization, or stemming if needed.
- **Behavior:**
  - o Outputs a list of tokens (e.g., ['this', 'is', 'a', 'sample', 'text']).
  - o Makes raw text compatible with machine learning models.
- **Output:** Tokenized text ready for vocabulary building or numericalization.

Example:
```
print(tokens)
```

Example Explanation:
- Logs the tokenized output for verification.
- Confirms successful text preprocessing.

2. Create Vocabulary

What is Vocabulary Creation?
A vocabulary maps tokens to unique numerical indices, enabling numerical representation of text data.

Syntax:
```
from torchtext.vocab import vocab
from collections import Counter
counter = Counter(tokens)
vocab = vocab(counter, max_size=1000)
```

Detailed Explanation:
- **Purpose:** Assigns a unique integer to each token, creating a numerical representation of the text corpus.
- **Parameters:**
  - o counter: A Counter object with token frequencies.
  - o max_size: Maximum size of the vocabulary to limit memory usage.

- **Behavior:**
  - Creates mappings like `{'this': 0, 'is': 1, 'a': 2, 'sample': 3, 'text': 4}`.
  - Adds special tokens such as `<unk>` for unknown words.
- **Output:** A vocabulary object with token-to-index and index-to-token mappings.

Example:
```
print(vocab['sample'])
```

Example Explanation:
- Retrieves the index of a specific token from the vocabulary.
- Ensures correct mapping of tokens to numerical indices.

3. Numericalize Tokens

What is Numericalization?

Numericalization converts tokens into numerical indices based on the vocabulary.

Syntax:
```
indices = [vocab[token] for token in tokens]
```

Detailed Explanation:
- **Purpose:** Transforms tokenized text into numerical format for model input.
- **Steps:**
  - Iterate through tokens and fetch their indices from the vocabulary.
  - Handle unknown tokens using a special `<unk>` index.
- **Behavior:**
  - Maps tokens to numbers (e.g., `['this', 'is']` -> `[0, 1]`).
  - Creates a numerical representation suitable for embeddings or models.
- **Output:** A list of integers corresponding to the input tokens.

Example:
```
print(indices)
```

Example Explanation:
- Logs the numerical indices for verification.
- Confirms alignment with the vocabulary.

4. Apply Embeddings

What are Embeddings?

Embeddings are dense vector representations of tokens that capture semantic relationships.

Syntax:

```
import torch.nn as nn

embedding = nn.Embedding(num_embeddings=len(vocab),
embedding_dim=50)
embedded_tokens = embedding(torch.tensor(indices))
```

Detailed Explanation:

- **Purpose:** Encodes tokens into fixed-size dense vectors.
- **Parameters:**
    - num_embeddings: Total number of tokens in the vocabulary.
    - embedding_dim: Dimensionality of the dense vector space.
- **Behavior:**
    - Transforms token indices into continuous vectors.
    - Captures semantic similarity between tokens.
- **Output:** A tensor of shape (`sequence_length, embedding_dim`).

Example:

```
print(embedded_tokens.shape)
```

Example Explanation:

- Logs the shape of the embedding tensor for verification.
- Confirms compatibility with downstream models.

5. Create DataLoader

What is a DataLoader?

A DataLoader batches and shuffles text data for efficient model training and evaluation.

Syntax:

```
from torch.utils.data import DataLoader, TensorDataset

data = TensorDataset(torch.tensor(indices),
torch.tensor(labels))
data_loader = DataLoader(data, batch_size=32,
shuffle=True)
```

Detailed Explanation:

- **Purpose:** Organizes data into manageable batches for training.
- **Parameters:**
  - TensorDataset: Combines features and labels into a single dataset.
  - batch_size: Number of samples per batch.
  - shuffle: Randomizes the order of samples.
- **Behavior:**
  - Groups text data into batches of uniform size.
  - Prepares data for efficient GPU processing.
- **Output:** An iterable data loader for training loops.

Example:

```
for batch in data_loader:
    print(batch)
```

Example Explanation:

- Displays batched text and labels for verification.
- Confirms correct batching and shuffling.

Real-Life Project:

Project Name: Text Classification with PyTorch

Project Goal: Build and train a sentiment analysis model using preprocessed text data.

Code for This Project:

```python
import torch
import torch.nn as nn
import torch.optim as optim
from torch.utils.data import DataLoader, TensorDataset
from torchtext.data.utils import get_tokenizer
from torchtext.vocab import vocab
from collections import Counter

# Step 1: Tokenize and preprocess text
tokenizer = get_tokenizer("basic_english")
raw_texts = ["This movie is great!", "I did not like
this movie."]
tokenized_texts = [tokenizer(text) for text in
raw_texts]

# Step 2: Build vocabulary
counter = Counter([token for tokens in tokenized_texts
for token in tokens])
vocab = vocab(counter, max_size=100)

# Step 3: Numericalize tokens
numericalized_texts = [torch.tensor([vocab[token] for
token in tokens]) for tokens in tokenized_texts]
labels = torch.tensor([1, 0])  # Positive: 1, Negative:
0

# Step 4: Create DataLoader
data =
TensorDataset(torch.nn.utils.rnn.pad_sequence(numerical
ized_texts, batch_first=True), labels)
data_loader = DataLoader(data, batch_size=2,
```

```python
                                      shuffle=True)

# Define a simple model
class SimpleClassifier(nn.Module):
    def __init__(self, vocab_size, embed_dim):
        super(SimpleClassifier, self).__init__()
        self.embedding = nn.Embedding(vocab_size,
embed_dim)
        self.fc = nn.Linear(embed_dim, 2)

    def forward(self, x):
        x = self.embedding(x).mean(dim=1)
        return self.fc(x)

model = SimpleClassifier(len(vocab), 50)
criterion = nn.CrossEntropyLoss()
optimizer = optim.Adam(model.parameters(), lr=0.001)

# Training loop
for epoch in range(5):
    for inputs, labels in data_loader:
        optimizer.zero_grad()
        outputs = model(inputs)
        loss = criterion(outputs, labels)
        loss.backward()
        optimizer.step()

    print(f"Epoch {epoch+1}, Loss: {loss.item():.4f}")

print("Training complete.")
```

Expected Output:

- Logs training loss for each epoch.
- Outputs a trained text classifier ready for evaluation.

Chapter - 34 Implementing RNNs and LSTMs in PyTorch

Recurrent Neural Networks (RNNs) and Long Short-Term Memory networks (LSTMs) are widely used for sequence modeling tasks such as text generation, machine translation, and time series analysis. PyTorch provides native modules and utilities to build and train RNNs and LSTMs effectively. This chapter introduces the basics of RNNs and LSTMs and demonstrates how to implement and train these models in PyTorch.

Key Characteristics of RNNs and LSTMs:

- **Sequential Modeling:** Designed to handle sequential data by maintaining temporal dependencies.
- **Hidden States:** RNNs maintain a hidden state to capture sequence context.
- **Memory Cells:** LSTMs improve RNNs by introducing memory cells that mitigate vanishing gradient issues.
- **Applications:** NLP, speech recognition, stock price prediction, and more.
- **Customizability:** Allows flexible architectures for diverse use cases.

Steps to Implement RNNs and LSTMs:

1. **Prepare Data:** Process sequential data and convert it to tensors.
2. **Define the Model:** Create RNN or LSTM architectures.
3. **Set Up Training Components:** Define the optimizer, loss function, and data loaders.
4. **Train the Model:** Train the model on the dataset and monitor performance.
5. **Evaluate the Model:** Test the model on unseen data and visualize results.

Syntax Table:

SL No	Function	Syntax/Example	Description
1	Define RNN	`nn.RNN(input_size, hidden_size, num_layers)`	Constructs a basic RNN layer.
2	Define LSTM	`nn.LSTM(input_size, hidden_size, num_layers)`	Constructs an LSTM layer.
3	Initialize Hidden State	`torch.zeros(num_layers, batch_size, hidden_size)`	Creates the initial hidden state for RNNs.
4	Forward Pass Through Model	`output, hidden = model(input, hidden)`	Processes input sequences through the model.
5	Train Model	`model.train()`	Switches the model to training mode.

Syntax Explanation:

1. Define RNN

What is an RNN?
An RNN processes sequential data by maintaining a hidden state that captures context from previous inputs.

Syntax:
```
import torch.nn as nn

rnn = nn.RNN(input_size=10, hidden_size=20,
num_layers=2, batch_first=True)
```

Detailed Explanation:
- **Purpose:** Models sequential dependencies in data.
- **Parameters:**
  - `input_size`: Number of features in the input sequence.
  - `hidden_size`: Number of features in the hidden state.

- o num_layers: Number of stacked RNN layers.
- o batch_first: If True, input and output tensors have shape (batch, seq, feature).
- **Behavior:**
  - o Takes a sequence as input and updates the hidden state for each time step.
  - o Outputs the hidden states and final state.
- **Output:** An RNN layer ready for sequential data processing.

Example:

```
print(rnn)
```

Example Explanation:

- Displays the architecture of the RNN layer.
- Confirms input size, hidden size, and number of layers.

2. Define LSTM

What is an LSTM?

An LSTM is an advanced RNN that includes memory cells to retain information over long sequences.

Syntax:

```
lstm = nn.LSTM(input_size=10, hidden_size=20,
num_layers=2, batch_first=True)
```

Detailed Explanation:

- **Purpose:** Improves upon RNNs by mitigating vanishing gradient issues with memory cells.
- **Parameters:**
  - o input_size: Number of features in the input sequence.
  - o hidden_size: Number of features in the hidden state.
  - o num_layers: Number of stacked LSTM layers.
  - o batch_first: If True, input and output tensors have shape (batch, seq, feature).
- **Behavior:**
  - o Uses gates (input, forget, and output) to control the flow of information.
  - o Outputs hidden states and cell states.
- **Output:** An LSTM layer ready for sequential data processing.

Example:
```
print(lstm)
```
Example Explanation:
- Displays the architecture of the LSTM layer.
- Confirms parameter settings for the LSTM.

3. Initialize Hidden State

What is a Hidden State?
The hidden state initializes the memory of the RNN or LSTM for the first time step.

Syntax:
```
hidden = torch.zeros(2, batch_size, 20)   # For 2-layer
RNN or LSTM
```

Detailed Explanation:
- **Purpose:** Provides initial values for the hidden state (and cell state for LSTMs).
- **Parameters:**
  - 2: Number of layers.
  - batch_size: Number of sequences in a batch.
  - 20: Hidden size, matching the hidden_size parameter of the model.
- **Behavior:**
  - Used to initialize the model's state before processing a sequence.
  - Ensures compatibility with the model's structure.
- **Output:** A tensor representing the initial hidden state.

Example:
```
print(hidden.shape)
```
Example Explanation:
- Logs the shape of the hidden state to ensure alignment with the model.

4. Forward Pass Through Model

What is a Forward Pass?
The forward pass processes input data through the RNN or LSTM to generate outputs and updated states.

Syntax:
```
output, hidden = rnn(input, hidden)
```
Detailed Explanation:
- **Purpose:** Passes sequential data through the model.
- **Parameters:**
  - input: Tensor of shape (`batch, seq_length, input_size`).
  - hidden: Initial hidden state (and cell state for LSTMs).
- **Behavior:**
  - Updates the hidden state for each time step.
  - Outputs:
    - output: Hidden states for all time steps.
    - hidden: Final hidden state (and cell state for LSTMs).
- **Output:**
  - A tuple containing the sequence of hidden states and the final state.

Example:
```
print(output.shape, hidden.shape)
```
Example Explanation:
- Verifies the dimensions of the outputs.
- Confirms the model processes input correctly.

5. Train Model

What is Training a Model?
Training involves updating the model's parameters to minimize a loss function over sequential data.

Syntax:
```
model.train()
for inputs, labels in data_loader:
    hidden = torch.zeros(2, inputs.size(0), 20)   #
```

```
Reset hidden state for each batch
    optimizer.zero_grad()
    outputs, hidden = model(inputs, hidden)
    loss = criterion(outputs, labels)
    loss.backward()
    optimizer.step()
```

Detailed Explanation:
- **Purpose:** Optimizes the model to improve predictions.
- **Steps:**
  - Reset the hidden state for each batch.
  - Perform a forward pass to compute predictions.
  - Calculate the loss between predictions and targets.
  - Update model parameters using backpropagation.
- **Output:** A trained RNN or LSTM model.

Example:
```
print(f"Loss: {loss.item():.4f}")
```
Example Explanation:
- Logs the training loss for each batch.
- Monitors model convergence.

Real-Life Project:

Project Name: Text Generation with LSTMs

Project Goal: Train an LSTM to generate text based on a corpus of Shakespeare's works.

Code for This Project:

```
import torch
import torch.nn as nn
import torch.optim as optim

# Define LSTM model
class TextGenerator(nn.Module):
    def __init__(self, vocab_size, embed_size,
hidden_size, num_layers):
        super(TextGenerator, self).__init__()
        self.embedding = nn.Embedding(vocab_size,
```

```python
        embed_size)
        self.lstm = nn.LSTM(embed_size, hidden_size,
num_layers, batch_first=True)
        self.fc = nn.Linear(hidden_size, vocab_size)

    def forward(self, x, hidden):
        x = self.embedding(x)
        out, hidden = self.lstm(x, hidden)
        out = self.fc(out)
        return out, hidden

# Instantiate the model
vocab_size = 1000
model = TextGenerator(vocab_size, embed_size=128,
hidden_size=256, num_layers=2)
criterion = nn.CrossEntropyLoss()
optimizer = optim.Adam(model.parameters(), lr=0.001)

# Training loop
for epoch in range(10):
    hidden = (torch.zeros(2, batch_size, 256),
torch.zeros(2, batch_size, 256))  # Initialize hidden
and cell states
    for inputs, labels in data_loader:
        optimizer.zero_grad()
        outputs, hidden = model(inputs, hidden)
        loss = criterion(outputs.view(-1, vocab_size),
labels.view(-1))
        loss.backward()
        optimizer.step()

    print(f"Epoch {epoch+1}, Loss: {loss.item():.4f}")
print("Training complete.")
```

Expected Output:
- Logs training loss for each epoch.
- Outputs a trained LSTM model capable of generating text.

Chapter – 35 Sentiment Analysis and Text Classification

Sentiment analysis and text classification are fundamental tasks in natural language processing (NLP) used to extract insights or categorize textual data. Sentiment analysis determines the emotional tone of text (e.g., positive, negative, or neutral), while text classification assigns predefined categories to text. PyTorch, with libraries like `torchtext` and `transformers`, simplifies building and training models for these tasks. This chapter covers the essential steps for implementing sentiment analysis and text classification in PyTorch.

Key Characteristics of Sentiment Analysis and Text Classification:
- **Task-Specific Models:** Can use custom architectures or pre-trained models like BERT.
- **Tokenization and Embedding:** Converts text into numerical format for model input.
- **Customizability:** Allows for tailored preprocessing, datasets, and model designs.
- **Applications:** Social media sentiment analysis, spam detection, topic categorization, etc.

Steps for Sentiment Analysis and Text Classification:
1. **Prepare the Dataset:** Tokenize and preprocess text data into numerical format.
2. **Choose an Architecture:** Select or design a model suitable for text classification tasks.
3. **Define Training Components:** Configure loss functions, optimizers, and evaluation metrics.
4. **Train the Model:** Train the model on labeled data and monitor performance.
5. **Evaluate and Test:** Test the model on unseen data to measure its effectiveness.
6. **Deploy:** Save and deploy the model for real-world use cases.

Syntax Table:

SL No	Function	Syntax/Example	Description
1	Tokenize Text	`tokenizer.encode(text, return_tensors='pt')`	Converts text into token IDs for model input.
2	Define Embedding Layer	`nn.Embedding(num_embeddings, embedding_dim)`	Maps tokens to dense vectors.
3	Define Model Architecture	`nn.Sequential(*layers)`	Constructs the neural network.
4	Define Loss Function	`nn.CrossEntropyLoss()`	Configures the loss function for classification.
5	Train Model	`model.train()`	Switches the model to training mode.

Syntax Explanation:

1. Tokenize Text

What is Tokenizing Text?
Tokenization converts raw text into a sequence of tokens, which are then converted into numerical IDs for model input.

Syntax:

```
from transformers import AutoTokenizer

tokenizer = AutoTokenizer.from_pretrained("bert-base-uncased")
tokens = tokenizer.encode("This is a sample text.", return_tensors='pt')
```

Detailed Explanation:

- **Purpose:** Prepares raw text for processing by NLP models.
- **Parameters:**
  - `text`: The input string to tokenize.
  - `return_tensors`: Specifies the output format (e.g., PyTorch tensor).
- **Behavior:**
  - Splits the text into subwords or tokens.
  - Converts tokens into numerical IDs.
- **Output:** Token IDs in tensor format ready for model input.

Example:
```
print(tokens)
```
Example Explanation:

- Displays the numerical representation of the input text.
- Ensures proper tokenization for compatibility with the model.

2. Define Embedding Layer

What is an Embedding Layer?
An embedding layer maps token IDs to dense vector representations that capture semantic meaning.

Syntax:
```
import torch.nn as nn
embedding = nn.Embedding(num_embeddings=10000,
embedding_dim=300)
```
Detailed Explanation:

- **Purpose:** Encodes discrete token IDs into continuous, dense vectors.
- **Parameters:**
  - `num_embeddings`: Size of the vocabulary.
  - `embedding_dim`: Dimensionality of the embedding vectors.
- **Behavior:**
  - Maps each token ID to a dense vector of fixed size.
  - Learns meaningful representations during training.
- **Output:** An embedding layer ready to process token IDs.

Example:
```
token_ids = torch.tensor([1, 2, 3])
embedded_tokens = embedding(token_ids)
print(embedded_tokens)
```
Example Explanation:
- Displays dense vector representations for token IDs.
- Verifies correct mapping of tokens to embeddings.

3. Define Model Architecture

What is Defining a Model Architecture?
Defining a model architecture involves specifying layers and connections for processing text data.
Syntax:
```
import torch.nn as nn
model = nn.Sequential(
    nn.Embedding(10000, 300),
    nn.LSTM(300, 128, batch_first=True),
    nn.Linear(128, num_classes)
)
```
Detailed Explanation:
- **Purpose:** Processes text embeddings and outputs predictions for classification.
- **Components:**
    o **nn.Embedding:** Converts token IDs to embeddings.
    o **nn.LSTM:** Captures sequential dependencies in text.
    o **nn.Linear:** Maps features to class probabilities.
- **Behavior:**
    o Encodes text features and aggregates contextual information.
    o Produces logits or probabilities for each class.
- **Output:** A sequential model for text classification.

Example:
```
print(model)
```
Example Explanation:
- Displays the architecture and configuration of the model.
- Confirms layer connections and output dimensions.

4. Define Loss Function

What is a Loss Function?
The loss function measures the error between predictions and true labels,
guiding the optimization process.
Syntax:
```
criterion = nn.CrossEntropyLoss()
```
Detailed Explanation:
- **Purpose:** Computes the difference between predicted
  probabilities and actual labels.
- **Parameters:**
  - Takes logits from the model and true labels as inputs.
- **Behavior:**
  - Assigns higher loss to incorrect predictions.
  - Guides the optimizer to reduce classification errors.
- **Output:** A scalar loss value for optimization.

Example:
```
logits = torch.tensor([[1.2, 0.8, 0.5], [0.2, 2.1,
0.3]])
labels = torch.tensor([0, 1])
loss = criterion(logits, labels)
print(loss.item())
```
Example Explanation:
- Computes the loss for a batch of predictions.
- Ensures the loss function aligns with the task requirements.

5. Train Model

What is Training a Model?
Training a model involves optimizing its parameters to minimize the loss
function over multiple iterations.
Syntax:
```
model.train()
for inputs, labels in data_loader:
    inputs, labels = inputs.to(device),
labels.to(device)
```

```
optimizer.zero_grad()
outputs = model(inputs)
loss = criterion(outputs, labels)
loss.backward()
optimizer.step()
```

Detailed Explanation:

- **Purpose:** Updates model parameters to improve classification accuracy.
- **Steps:**
  - Sets the model to training mode with `model.train()`.
  - Processes batches of tokenized text and corresponding labels.
  - Computes predictions, calculates loss, and updates parameters.
- **Output:** An optimized model ready for evaluation.

Example:
```
print(f"Loss: {loss.item():.4f}")
```

Example Explanation:

- Logs the loss for each batch, allowing monitoring of training progress.

Real-Life Project:

Project Name: Sentiment Analysis of Movie Reviews

Project Goal: Build a model to classify movie reviews as positive or negative using transfer learning with BERT.

Code for This Project:

```
from transformers import
AutoModelForSequenceClassification, AutoTokenizer
import torch
from torch.utils.data import DataLoader


# Load pre-trained BERT model and tokenizer
model =
AutoModelForSequenceClassification.from_pretrained("ber
t-base-uncased", num_labels=2)
tokenizer = AutoTokenizer.from_pretrained("bert-base-
```

```
uncased")

# Prepare dataset
def encode_batch(batch):
    return tokenizer(batch["text"], padding=True,
truncation=True, return_tensors="pt")

# Example data
data = [{"text": "This movie was fantastic!", "label":
1},
        {"text": "The movie was terrible.", "label":
0}]

# Tokenize data
inputs = encode_batch(data)
labels = torch.tensor([d["label"] for d in data])

# Training components
criterion = torch.nn.CrossEntropyLoss()
optimizer = torch.optim.Adam(model.parameters(), lr=2e-
5)

# Training loop
model.train()
for epoch in range(3):
    optimizer.zero_grad()
    outputs = model(**inputs)
    loss = criterion(outputs.logits, labels)
    loss.backward()
    optimizer.step()
    print(f"Epoch {epoch+1}, Loss: {loss.item():.4f}")
print("Training complete.")
```

Expected Output:
- Logs training loss for each epoch.
- Outputs a fine-tuned BERT model ready for sentiment classification.

Chapter - 36 Machine Translation Using PyTorch

Machine translation is the task of converting text from one language to another using models trained on bilingual datasets. PyTorch provides the flexibility to build custom architectures for sequence-to-sequence tasks, as well as pre-trained models through libraries like `transformers`. This chapter explores how to implement machine translation models using PyTorch, covering both custom and pre-trained approaches.

Key Characteristics of Machine Translation Models:

- **Sequence-to-Sequence (Seq2Seq):** Common architecture involving an encoder-decoder structure.
- **Attention Mechanisms:** Enhances translation quality by focusing on relevant parts of the input sequence.
- **Pre-trained Models:** Includes models like MarianMT and mBART for efficient translation.
- **Customizability:** Enables building and training models tailored to specific language pairs or domains.
- **Applications:** Cross-language communication, localization, and multilingual NLP tasks.

Steps for Machine Translation:

1. **Prepare the Dataset:** Load and preprocess bilingual text pairs.
2. **Choose an Architecture:** Select between custom Seq2Seq models or pre-trained models.
3. **Define Training Components:** Configure loss functions, optimizers, and evaluation metrics.
4. **Train the Model:** Train the translation model on paired data.
5. **Evaluate and Test:** Test the model on unseen data and compute metrics like BLEU score.
6. **Deploy:** Save the model and deploy it for real-time or batch translation tasks.

Syntax Table:

SL No	Function	Syntax/Example	Description
1	Load Pre-trained Model	`AutoModelForSeq2SeqLM.from_pretrained(model_name)`	Loads a pre-trained sequence-to-sequence model.
2	Tokenize Input Text	`tokenizer(text, return_tensors='pt')`	Converts text into token IDs for model input.
3	Define Custom Encoder-Decoder	`nn.LSTM(input_size, hidden_size, num_layers)`	Constructs a custom Seq2Seq architecture.
4	Translate Text	`model.generate(input_ids)`	Generates translations using the trained model.
5	Compute BLEU Score	`nltk.translate.bleu_score.sentence_bleu`	Evaluates the quality of generated translations.

Syntax Explanation:

1. Load Pre-trained Model

What is Loading a Pre-trained Model?
Pre-trained models simplify translation tasks by leveraging large-scale training on multilingual datasets.

Syntax:
```
from transformers import AutoModelForSeq2SeqLM
model =
AutoModelForSeq2SeqLM.from_pretrained("Helsinki-
NLP/opus-mt-en-de")
```
Detailed Explanation:
- **Purpose:** Provides a pre-trained encoder-decoder model for translation.
- **Parameters:**

- o model_name: Specifies the pre-trained model to load (e.g., "Helsinki-NLP/opus-mt-en-de").
- **Behavior:**
  - o Loads the model architecture and weights.
  - o Outputs a model ready for inference or fine-tuning.
- **Output:** A pre-trained model for English-to-German translation.

Example:
```
print(model.config)
```
Example Explanation:
- Displays the configuration of the loaded model.
- Confirms compatibility with the desired task.

2. Tokenize Input Text

What is Tokenizing Input Text?
Tokenization converts raw text into numerical IDs that the model can process.

Syntax:
```
from transformers import AutoTokenizer

tokenizer = AutoTokenizer.from_pretrained("Helsinki-
NLP/opus-mt-en-de")
input_ids = tokenizer("Translate this sentence.",
return_tensors='pt')
```
Detailed Explanation:
- **Purpose:** Prepares text data for translation by encoding it into model-compatible inputs.
- **Parameters:**
  - o text: Input string to be translated.
  - o return_tensors: Specifies the output format (e.g., PyTorch tensor).
- **Behavior:**
  - o Splits the text into tokens and converts them into numerical IDs.
  - o Appends special tokens as required by the model.
- **Output:** Token IDs in tensor format ready for model inference.

Example:
```
print(input_ids)
```
Example Explanation:

- Displays the tokenized representation of the input text.
- Verifies proper tokenization.

3. Define Custom Encoder-Decoder

What is a Custom Encoder-Decoder?

A custom encoder-decoder processes input sequences and generates corresponding output sequences.

Syntax:
```
import torch.nn as nn

class Seq2SeqModel(nn.Module):
    def __init__(self, input_dim, output_dim,
hidden_dim):
        super(Seq2SeqModel, self).__init__()
        self.encoder = nn.LSTM(input_dim, hidden_dim,
batch_first=True)
        self.decoder = nn.LSTM(output_dim, hidden_dim,
batch_first=True)
        self.fc = nn.Linear(hidden_dim, output_dim)

    def forward(self, src, trg):
        _, (hidden, _) = self.encoder(src)
        outputs, _ = self.decoder(trg, (hidden,
torch.zeros_like(hidden)))
        return self.fc(outputs)
```
Detailed Explanation:

- **Purpose:** Defines a Seq2Seq architecture with LSTM layers for translation.
- **Components:**
    ○ **nn.LSTM:** Encodes input sequences and decodes outputs sequentially.
    ○ **nn.Linear:** Maps decoder outputs to the target vocabulary space.

- **Behavior:**
  - ○ Processes source text through the encoder to create a context vector.
  - ○ Generates translations by decoding the context vector into the target language.
- **Output:** A model that learns mappings between source and target sequences.

Example:
```
print(Seq2SeqModel(128, 128, 256))
```
Example Explanation:
- Displays the structure of the custom Seq2Seq model.
- Confirms compatibility with input-output dimensions.

4. Translate Text

What is Translating Text?
Translating text uses the trained or pre-trained model to generate output sequences in the target language.

Syntax:
```
output_ids = model.generate(input_ids["input_ids"])
translated_text = tokenizer.decode(output_ids[0],
skip_special_tokens=True)
```
Detailed Explanation:
- **Purpose:** Produces translations from tokenized input sequences.
- **Steps:**
  - ○ Passes tokenized input through the model.
  - ○ Decodes the output token IDs into readable text.
- **Output:** Translated text in the target language.

Example:
```
print(translated_text)
```
Example Explanation:
- Outputs the translated sentence.
- Verifies model performance on a sample input.

5. Compute BLEU Score

What is a BLEU Score?
The BLEU (Bilingual Evaluation Understudy) score evaluates the quality of machine-generated translations by comparing them to reference translations.
Syntax:
```
from nltk.translate.bleu_score import sentence_bleu

reference = ["Das ist ein Beispielsatz."]
candidate = "Dies ist ein Beispielsatz."
bleu_score = sentence_bleu([reference],
candidate.split())
```
Detailed Explanation:
- **Purpose:** Measures the similarity between the candidate translation and the reference.
- **Parameters:**
    o   reference: List of ground truth translations.
    o   candidate: Model-generated translation.
- **Behavior:**
    o   Computes a similarity score based on n-gram overlap.
    o   Scores range from 0 (no overlap) to 1 (perfect match).
- **Output:** A numerical BLEU score for the translation quality.

Example:
```
print(f"BLEU Score: {bleu_score:.2f}")
```
Example Explanation:
- Logs the BLEU score for the candidate translation.
- Helps evaluate model performance.

Real-Life Project:
Project Name: English-to-German Neural Machine Translation
Project Goal: Build a translation pipeline using a pre-trained MarianMT model for English-to-German translation.

Code for This Project:

```python
from transformers import MarianMTModel, MarianTokenizer

# Load pre-trained MarianMT model and tokenizer
model_name = "Helsinki-NLP/opus-mt-en-de"
model = MarianMTModel.from_pretrained(model_name)
tokenizer = MarianTokenizer.from_pretrained(model_name)

# Prepare input text
text = "How are you today?"
input_ids = tokenizer(text, return_tensors="pt",
padding=True, truncation=True)

# Generate translation
output_ids = model.generate(input_ids["input_ids"])
translated_text = tokenizer.decode(output_ids[0],
skip_special_tokens=True)

print("Input:", text)
print("Translation:", translated_text)
```

Expected Output:

- Logs the input text and its German translation.
- Demonstrates the ease of using pre-trained models for translation.

Chapter - 37 Time Series Forecasting with PyTorch

Time series forecasting involves predicting future values based on historical data. It is widely used in various fields such as finance, weather prediction, and demand forecasting. PyTorch provides flexible tools for building, training, and evaluating time series models, including custom architectures and pre-trained solutions. This chapter explores methods to implement time series forecasting using PyTorch, covering preprocessing, model design, and evaluation.

Key Characteristics of Time Series Forecasting Models:
- **Sequential Data Handling:** Models process data with inherent temporal dependencies.
- **Customizability:** Allows designing specific architectures such as RNNs, LSTMs, GRUs, and Transformers.
- **Scalability:** Can handle varying sequence lengths and multivariate data.
- **Evaluation Metrics:** Uses metrics like MAE (Mean Absolute Error) and RMSE (Root Mean Squared Error) for assessment.
- **Applications:** Stock price prediction, anomaly detection, energy usage forecasting, and more.

Steps for Time Series Forecasting:
1. **Prepare the Dataset:** Normalize and structure the data into sequences.
2. **Choose a Model Architecture:** Select or design models such as LSTM, GRU, or Transformer.
3. **Define Training Components:** Set up loss functions, optimizers, and learning rate schedules.
4. **Train the Model:** Train the model on historical data and monitor loss.
5. **Evaluate the Model:** Test on unseen data and calculate evaluation metrics.
6. **Deploy:** Save the model and deploy it for real-time forecasting tasks.

Syntax Table:

SL No	Function	Syntax/Example	Description
1	Load and Prepare Data	`torch.utils.data.DataLoader(dataset, batch_size)`	Prepares data loaders for training and testing.
2	Define LSTM Model	`nn.LSTM(input_size, hidden_size, num_layers)`	Constructs an LSTM for sequential data.
3	Define Loss Function	`nn.MSELoss()`	Configures the loss function for regression tasks.
4	Train the Model	`model.train()`	Switches the model to training mode.
5	Evaluate the Model	`model.eval()`	Switches the model to evaluation mode.

Syntax Explanation:

1. Load and Prepare Data

What is Loading and Preparing Data?
Loading and preparing time series data involves organizing it into sequences for training and testing.
Syntax:

```
import torch
from torch.utils.data import DataLoader, TensorDataset

# Sample data preparation
data = torch.arange(1, 101).float()  # Example time
series data
sequence_length = 10
sequences = [data[i:i+sequence_length] for i in
```

```
range(len(data) - sequence_length)]
data_x = torch.stack([seq[:-1] for seq in sequences])
# Inputs
data_y = torch.stack([seq[-1] for seq in sequences])
# Targets

dataset = TensorDataset(data_x, data_y)
data_loader = DataLoader(dataset, batch_size=16,
shuffle=True)
```

Detailed Explanation:

- **Purpose:** Structures data into input-output pairs for supervised learning.
- **Components:**
  - **data:** Time series values.
  - **sequence_length:** Number of time steps in each sequence.
  - **TensorDataset:** Creates a dataset from input-output pairs.
  - **DataLoader:** Provides batching and shuffling for training.
- **Behavior:**
  - Splits the time series into overlapping sequences.
  - Divides the sequences into inputs (data_x) and targets (data_y).
- **Output:** A data loader for model training.

Example:

```
print(f"Input Shape: {data_x.shape}, Target Shape:
{data_y.shape}")
```

Example Explanation:

- Logs the dimensions of the inputs and targets to verify correctness.

2. Define LSTM Model

What is an LSTM Model?

An LSTM (Long Short-Term Memory) model captures long-term dependencies in sequential data.

Syntax:

```
import torch.nn as nn

class LSTMModel(nn.Module):
    def __init__(self, input_size, hidden_size,
num_layers, output_size):
        super(LSTMModel, self).__init__()
        self.lstm = nn.LSTM(input_size, hidden_size,
num_layers, batch_first=True)
        self.fc = nn.Linear(hidden_size, output_size)

    def forward(self, x):
        _, (hidden, _) = self.lstm(x)
        return self.fc(hidden[-1])
model = LSTMModel(input_size=1, hidden_size=32,
num_layers=2, output_size=1)
```

Detailed Explanation:

- **Purpose:** Processes sequential data and predicts the next value.
- **Components:**
  - **nn.LSTM:** Encodes the input sequence into a hidden state.
  - **nn.Linear:** Maps the hidden state to the output dimension.
- **Behavior:**
  - Takes input sequences and generates predictions for the next time step.
- **Output:** A PyTorch model ready for training.

Example:

```
print(model)
```

Example Explanation:

- Displays the architecture of the LSTM model.
- Confirms the compatibility of input-output dimensions.

3. Define Loss Function

What is a Loss Function?

The loss function measures the difference between predicted and actual values, guiding model optimization.

Syntax:

```
criterion = nn.MSELoss()
```

Detailed Explanation:

- **Purpose:** Computes the Mean Squared Error between predictions and targets.
- **Behavior:**
    - Penalizes large deviations between predicted and true values.
    - Guides the optimizer to minimize prediction errors.
- **Output:** A scalar loss value for optimization.

Example:

```
predictions = torch.tensor([2.5, 3.5])
actuals = torch.tensor([3.0, 4.0])
loss = criterion(predictions, actuals)
print(f"Loss: {loss.item():.4f}")
```

Example Explanation:

- Logs the computed loss for a batch of predictions and targets.

4. Train the Model

What is Training a Model?

Training a model involves iteratively optimizing its parameters to minimize the loss function.

Syntax:

```
model.train()
for inputs, targets in data_loader:
    inputs, targets = inputs.unsqueeze(-1),
targets.unsqueeze(-1)  # Add feature dimension
    optimizer.zero_grad()
    outputs = model(inputs)
    loss = criterion(outputs, targets)
    loss.backward()
```

```
optimizer.step()
```
Detailed Explanation:

- **Purpose:** Updates model weights to improve predictions.
- **Steps:**
    - Switches the model to training mode with `model.train()`.
    - Processes batches of input-output pairs.
    - Computes predictions, calculates loss, and updates weights.
- **Output:** A trained model ready for evaluation.

Example:
```
print(f"Training Loss: {loss.item():.4f}")
```
Example Explanation:

- Logs the loss for each batch, enabling monitoring of training progress.

5. Evaluate the Model

What is Evaluating a Model?

Evaluating a model tests its performance on unseen data and computes relevant metrics.

Syntax:
```
model.eval()
with torch.no_grad():
    for inputs, targets in test_loader:
        inputs, targets = inputs.unsqueeze(-1),
targets.unsqueeze(-1)
        predictions = model(inputs)
        loss = criterion(predictions, targets)
```
Detailed Explanation:

- **Purpose:** Measures the model's accuracy and generalization capability.
- **Steps:**
    - Switches the model to evaluation mode with `model.eval()`.
    - Disables gradient computation using `torch.no_grad()`.
    - Processes test data and computes metrics.

- **Output:** Evaluation metrics like MAE or RMSE.

Example:

```
print(f"Evaluation Loss: {loss.item():.4f}")
```

Example Explanation:

- Logs the evaluation loss for the test dataset.

Real-Life Project:

Project Name: Stock Price Forecasting with LSTM

Project Goal: Build and train an LSTM model to predict stock prices based on historical data.

Code for This Project:

```python
import torch
import torch.nn as nn
import torch.optim as optim
from torch.utils.data import DataLoader, TensorDataset

# Data preparation
data = torch.linspace(1, 100, steps=100).float()
sequence_length = 10
sequences = [data[i:i+sequence_length] for i in
range(len(data) - sequence_length)]
data_x = torch.stack([seq[:-1] for seq in sequences])
data_y = torch.stack([seq[-1] for seq in sequences])

dataset = TensorDataset(data_x.unsqueeze(-1),
data_y.unsqueeze(-1))
data_loader = DataLoader(dataset, batch_size=16,
shuffle=True)

# Define model
model = LSTMModel(input_size=1, hidden_size=32,
num_layers=2, output_size=1)
criterion = nn.MSELoss()
optimizer = optim.Adam(model.parameters(), lr=0.001)

# Training loop
```

```
for epoch in range(20):
    model.train()
    for inputs, targets in data_loader:
        optimizer.zero_grad()
        outputs = model(inputs)
        loss = criterion(outputs, targets)
        loss.backward()
        optimizer.step()

    print(f"Epoch {epoch+1}, Loss: {loss.item():.4f}")

print("Training complete.")
```

Expected Output:

- Logs training loss for each epoch.
- Outputs a trained model ready for time series forecasting tasks.

Chapter - 38 Basics of Reinforcement Learning with PyTorch

Reinforcement learning (RL) is a machine learning paradigm where agents learn to make decisions by interacting with an environment. Using PyTorch, RL models can be implemented efficiently with customizable components. This chapter explores the foundational concepts of RL, including key terminologies, algorithms like Q-learning and policy gradients, and their implementation in PyTorch.

Key Characteristics of Reinforcement Learning:

- **Agent-Environment Interaction:** Agents learn policies by taking actions and receiving feedback (rewards).
- **State-Action-Reward Framework:** Central to defining the RL problem.
- **Exploration vs. Exploitation:** Balances trying new actions and optimizing known rewards.
- **Algorithms:** Includes value-based methods (e.g., Q-learning) and policy-based methods (e.g., REINFORCE).
- **Applications:** Robotics, game AI, autonomous systems, and resource management.

Steps for Reinforcement Learning:

1. **Define the Environment:** Set up an environment where the agent operates.
2. **Build the Agent:** Design a model to map states to actions.
3. **Choose an Algorithm:** Select an RL algorithm (e.g., Q-learning, policy gradient).
4. **Train the Agent:** Use interaction data to improve the agent's policy.
5. **Evaluate and Fine-Tune:** Assess agent performance and refine the policy.

Syntax Table:

SL No	Function	Syntax/Example	Description
1	Create Environment	`gym.make(env_name)`	Sets up the simulation environment.
2	Define Q-Network	`nn.Sequential(*layers)`	Constructs a neural network for Q-value estimation.
3	Select Action	`epsilon_greedy_policy(q_values, epsilon)`	Chooses actions based on an epsilon-greedy policy.
4	Update Q-values	`q_update = reward + gamma * max_q_next`	Computes Q-value updates for learning.
5	Train Policy	`optimizer.step()`	Updates the agent's parameters.

Syntax Explanation:

1. Create Environment

What is Creating an Environment?
An environment provides the simulation where the agent interacts and learns.
Syntax:
```
import gym
env = gym.make("CartPole-v1")
state = env.reset()
```
Detailed Explanation:
- **Purpose:** Sets up a simulation with states, actions, and rewards.
- **Parameters:**
  - env_name: The name of the environment (e.g., "CartPole-v1").
- **Behavior:**
  - Initializes the environment.

- o   Resets it to its initial state.
- **Output:** The environment object and the initial state.

Example:
```
print(f"Initial State: {state}")
```
Example Explanation:
- Logs the initial state to confirm proper environment setup.

2. Define Q-Network

What is a Q-Network?
A Q-network estimates the Q-values (state-action values) for reinforcement learning tasks.

Syntax:
```
import torch.nn as nn

q_network = nn.Sequential(
    nn.Linear(input_dim, 128),
    nn.ReLU(),
    nn.Linear(128, num_actions)
)
```
Detailed Explanation:
- **Purpose:** Predicts Q-values for each action given a state.
- **Components:**
  - o   **nn.Linear:** Fully connected layers map inputs to outputs.
  - o   **nn.ReLU:** Introduces non-linearity.
- **Behavior:**
  - o   Processes input states through the network.
  - o   Outputs Q-values for all possible actions.
- **Output:** A PyTorch model for Q-value estimation.

Example:
```
print(q_network)
```
Example Explanation:
- Displays the architecture of the Q-network.
- Verifies input and output dimensions.

3. Select Action

What is Action Selection?

Action selection determines which action the agent takes in a given state.

Syntax:

```python
import torch
import random

def epsilon_greedy_policy(q_values, epsilon):
    if random.random() < epsilon:
        return random.randint(0, len(q_values) - 1)  # Explore
    else:
        return torch.argmax(q_values).item()  # Exploit

q_values = torch.tensor([1.2, 0.8, 0.5])
action = epsilon_greedy_policy(q_values, epsilon=0.1)
```

Detailed Explanation:

- **Purpose:** Balances exploration and exploitation during learning.
- **Parameters:**
    - `q_values`: Predicted Q-values for actions in the current state.
    - `epsilon`: Probability of choosing a random action.
- **Behavior:**
    - Explores randomly with probability `epsilon`.
    - Exploits the best action (highest Q-value) otherwise.
- **Output:** Selected action index.

Example:

```python
print(f"Selected Action: {action}")
```

Example Explanation:

- Logs the chosen action index based on the policy.

4. Update Q-values

What is Updating Q-values?
Q-value updates incorporate new information from the environment to improve decision-making.
Syntax:

```
def update_q_values(q_values, action, reward,
next_q_values, gamma):
    max_next_q = torch.max(next_q_values).item()
    q_values[action] = reward + gamma * max_next_q


q_values = torch.zeros(num_actions)
next_q_values = torch.tensor([1.5, 2.0, 0.5])
update_q_values(q_values, action=1, reward=1,
next_q_values=next_q_values, gamma=0.99)
```

Detailed Explanation:
- **Purpose:** Refines Q-values based on observed rewards and future predictions.
- **Parameters:**
  - reward: Immediate reward received.
  - gamma: Discount factor for future rewards.
- **Behavior:**
  - Computes the Bellman equation for Q-value updates.
  - Adjusts Q-values to better reflect long-term rewards.
- **Output:** Updated Q-values.

Example:

```
print(f"Updated Q-values: {q_values}")
```

Example Explanation:
- Logs the Q-values after updates to track learning progress.

5. Train Policy

What is Training a Policy?
Training a policy optimizes the agent's decision-making strategy to maximize rewards.

Syntax:

```
optimizer = torch.optim.Adam(q_network.parameters(),
lr=0.001)

q_network.train()
for state, action, reward, next_state in replay_buffer:
    q_values = q_network(state)
    next_q_values = q_network(next_state).detach()
    q_target = reward + gamma *
torch.max(next_q_values)

    loss = nn.MSELoss()(q_values[action], q_target)
    optimizer.zero_grad()
    loss.backward()
    optimizer.step()
```

Detailed Explanation:
- **Purpose:** Refines the Q-network to improve the agent's policy.
- **Steps:**
    - Predicts Q-values for the current state.
    - Computes the target Q-value using the Bellman equation.
    - Optimizes the network to minimize the loss between predicted and target Q-values.
- **Output:** An optimized Q-network.

Example:

```
print(f"Training Loss: {loss.item():.4f}")
```

Example Explanation:
- Logs the training loss to monitor convergence.

Real-Life Project:

Project Name: Training a CartPole Balancer with Q-Learning

Project Goal: Train an agent to balance a pole on a cart using Q-learning with a neural network.

Code for This Project:

```python
import gym
import torch
import torch.nn as nn
import torch.optim as optim
import random


# Define Q-network
class QNetwork(nn.Module):
    def __init__(self, input_dim, output_dim):
        super(QNetwork, self).__init__()
        self.net = nn.Sequential(
            nn.Linear(input_dim, 128),
            nn.ReLU(),
            nn.Linear(128, output_dim)
        )

    def forward(self, x):
        return self.net(x)


# Environment and model setup
env = gym.make("CartPole-v1")
q_network = \
QNetwork(input_dim=env.observation_space.shape[0],
output_dim=env.action_space.n)
optimizer = optim.Adam(q_network.parameters(),
lr=0.001)

epsilon, gamma = 0.1, 0.99


# Training loop
for episode in range(100):
```

```python
    state = env.reset()
    total_reward = 0
    for t in range(200):
        state_tensor = torch.tensor(state,
dtype=torch.float32)
        q_values = q_network(state_tensor)
        action = epsilon_greedy_policy(q_values,
epsilon)

        next_state, reward, done, _ = env.step(action)
        total_reward += reward

        # Q-value update
        next_state_tensor = torch.tensor(next_state,
dtype=torch.float32)
        next_q_values =
q_network(next_state_tensor).detach()
        q_target = reward + gamma *
torch.max(next_q_values)

        loss = nn.MSELoss()(q_values[action], q_target)
        optimizer.zero_grad()
        loss.backward()
        optimizer.step()

        if done:
            break
        state = next_state

    print(f"Episode {episode+1}, Total Reward:
{total_reward}")

print("Training complete.")
```
Expected Output:

- Logs total rewards per episode.
- Trains an agent capable of balancing the CartPole effectively.

Chapter - 39 Predicting House Prices with PyTorch

Predicting house prices is a classic regression problem where the goal is to predict a continuous target variable based on various input features (e.g., square footage, number of rooms, location). PyTorch provides a powerful framework for implementing and training regression models efficiently. This chapter outlines how to preprocess data, design models, and train a PyTorch-based solution for predicting house prices.

Key Characteristics of House Price Prediction Models:
- **Regression Task:** Outputs a continuous value as opposed to a categorical class.
- **Feature Engineering:** Requires preprocessing numerical and categorical features for optimal performance.
- **Scalability:** Handles large datasets effectively with data loaders.
- **Customizability:** Allows for designing custom architectures tailored to the dataset.
- **Evaluation Metrics:** Common metrics include Mean Squared Error (MSE) and Mean Absolute Error (MAE).

Steps for Predicting House Prices:
1. **Prepare the Dataset:** Preprocess features and split the data into training, validation, and test sets.
2. **Define the Model Architecture:** Design a neural network suitable for regression tasks.
3. **Define the Loss Function and Optimizer:** Configure the regression loss (e.g., MSELoss) and optimization strategy.
4. **Train the Model:** Train the model on the training set and monitor performance on the validation set.
5. **Evaluate and Test:** Assess the model's performance using metrics like MSE and MAE.
6. **Deploy:** Save the model for inference on new data.

Syntax Table:

SL No	Function	Syntax/Example	Description
1	Load Dataset	`pd.read_csv('data.csv')`	Loads tabular data from a CSV file.
2	Normalize Features	`(X - X.mean()) / X.std()`	Standardizes numerical features.
3	Define Model Architecture	`nn.Sequential(*layers)`	Constructs the neural network.
4	Define Loss Function	`nn.MSELoss()`	Configures the loss function for regression.
5	Train Model	`model.train()`	Switches the model to training mode.

Syntax Explanation:

1. Load Dataset

What is Loading a Dataset?
Loading a dataset involves importing the data from an external source into a format suitable for model training.

Syntax:
```
import pandas as pd
data = pd.read_csv("house_prices.csv")
```

Detailed Explanation:
- **Purpose:** Imports tabular data for analysis and preprocessing.
- **Parameters:**
  - `file_path`: Path to the CSV file containing the dataset.
- **Behavior:**
  - Reads the data into a Pandas DataFrame.
  - Provides functionalities to inspect, manipulate, and preprocess the data.
- **Output:** A DataFrame containing the dataset.

Example:
```
print(data.head())
```
Example Explanation:
- Displays the first few rows of the dataset for inspection.
- Ensures the data has been loaded correctly.

2. Normalize Features

What is Normalizing Features?
Normalization scales numerical features to have a mean of 0 and a standard deviation of 1.

Syntax:
```
X_normalized = (X - X.mean()) / X.std()
```
Detailed Explanation:
- **Purpose:** Ensures numerical stability and improves model convergence.
- **Process:**
  - Subtracts the mean from each feature.
  - Divides by the standard deviation.
- **Behavior:**
  - Transforms features into a standard scale.
  - Reduces the effect of varying scales in the dataset.
- **Output:** Normalized features.

Example:
```
X = data.drop(columns="price")
X_normalized = (X - X.mean()) / X.std()
print(X_normalized.head())
```

Example Explanation:
- Displays normalized features to verify the transformation.

3. Define Model Architecture

What is Defining a Model Architecture?
The model architecture specifies the layers and connections for processing input features and producing predictions.

Syntax:

```
import torch.nn as nn

model = nn.Sequential(
    nn.Linear(input_dim, 128),
    nn.ReLU(),
    nn.Linear(128, 64),
    nn.ReLU(),
    nn.Linear(64, 1)
)
```
Detailed Explanation:
- **Purpose:** Encodes the relationship between input features and the target variable.
- **Components:**
    - **nn.Linear:** Fully connected layers for feature transformation.
    - **nn.ReLU:** Activation function introducing non-linearity.
- **Behavior:**
    - Processes input features through layers.
    - Outputs a single continuous value for regression.
- **Output:** A neural network model ready for training.

Example:
```
print(model)
```
Example Explanation:
- Displays the architecture of the neural network.
- Verifies the layer configurations and dimensions.

4. Define Loss Function

What is a Loss Function?
A loss function measures the difference between predicted and actual target values, guiding the optimization process.

Syntax:
```
criterion = nn.MSELoss()
```
Detailed Explanation:
- **Purpose:** Quantifies the error in regression predictions.
- **Behavior:**
    - Computes the mean squared error between predictions

and true values.

- o Penalizes larger errors more heavily.
- **Output:** A scalar loss value for optimization.

Example:

```
predictions = torch.tensor([250000.0, 300000.0])
true_values = torch.tensor([240000.0, 310000.0])
loss = criterion(predictions, true_values)
print(f"Loss: {loss.item():.4f}")
```

Example Explanation:

- Computes the loss for a batch of predictions.
- Confirms the loss function is working correctly.

5. Train Model

What is Training a Model?

Training a model involves optimizing its parameters to minimize the loss function over several iterations.

Syntax:

```
model.train()
for inputs, labels in data_loader:
    inputs, labels = inputs.to(device),
labels.to(device)

    optimizer.zero_grad()
    outputs = model(inputs)
    loss = criterion(outputs, labels)
    loss.backward()
    optimizer.step()
```

Detailed Explanation:

- **Purpose:** Refines the model's predictions by iteratively updating parameters.
- **Steps:**
  - o Sets the model to training mode.
  - o Processes input batches through the model.
  - o Calculates loss and updates parameters.
- **Output:** A trained model ready for evaluation.

Example:

```
print(f"Loss: {loss.item():.4f}")
```
Example Explanation:
- Logs the loss for each batch, tracking training progress.

Real-Life Project:
Project Name: House Price Prediction Model
Project Goal: Build and train a neural network to predict house prices based on features such as square footage, location, and number of rooms.

Code for This Project:

```
import torch
import torch.nn as nn
import torch.optim as optim
from torch.utils.data import DataLoader, TensorDataset
import pandas as pd

# Load dataset
data = pd.read_csv("house_prices.csv")
X = data.drop(columns="price")
y = data["price"]

# Normalize features
X_normalized = (X - X.mean()) / X.std()
X_tensor = torch.tensor(X_normalized.values,
dtype=torch.float32)
y_tensor = torch.tensor(y.values,
dtype=torch.float32).unsqueeze(1)

# Create DataLoader
dataset = TensorDataset(X_tensor, y_tensor)
data_loader = DataLoader(dataset, batch_size=32,
shuffle=True)

# Define model
input_dim = X_tensor.shape[1]
model = nn.Sequential(
```

```python
    nn.Linear(input_dim, 128),
    nn.ReLU(),
    nn.Linear(128, 64),
    nn.ReLU(),
    nn.Linear(64, 1)
)

# Define optimizer and loss function
criterion = nn.MSELoss()
optimizer = optim.Adam(model.parameters(), lr=0.001)

# Training loop
for epoch in range(50):
    model.train()
    for inputs, labels in data_loader:
        optimizer.zero_grad()
        outputs = model(inputs)
        loss = criterion(outputs, labels)
        loss.backward()
        optimizer.step()

    print(f"Epoch {epoch+1}, Loss: {loss.item():.4f}")

print("Training complete.")
```

Expected Output:

- Logs the loss for each epoch.
- Outputs a trained model capable of predicting house prices accurately.

Chapter - 40 Creating a Real-Time Object Detector

A real-time object detector identifies and localizes objects within images or video streams with low latency. PyTorch, in conjunction with `torchvision` and hardware accelerators like GPUs, facilitates the development of real-time object detection systems. This chapter explores the steps to build, train, and deploy an efficient object detector capable of handling real-time applications such as surveillance, autonomous driving, and augmented reality.

Key Characteristics of Real-Time Object Detection Systems:

- **Speed and Efficiency:** Optimized for low-latency inference on hardware like GPUs.
- **State-of-the-Art Models:** Uses pre-trained models such as YOLO, SSD, or Faster R-CNN.
- **Customizability:** Adapts pre-trained models to custom datasets and tasks.
- **Dataset Compatibility:** Supports COCO, Pascal VOC, and custom datasets.
- **Real-Time Deployment:** Integrates with live video streams and edge devices.

Steps to Create a Real-Time Object Detector:

1. **Prepare the Dataset:** Load and preprocess labeled images for training.
2. **Select a Pre-trained Model:** Use models like Faster R-CNN or SSD from `torchvision.models.detection`.
3. **Fine-Tune the Model:** Adapt the model to a specific dataset and task.
4. **Optimize for Real-Time:** Use techniques like quantization and GPU acceleration.
5. **Deploy:** Integrate the trained model with a live video stream for real-time detection.

Syntax Table:

SL No	Function	Syntax/Example	Description
1	Load Dataset	`datasets.CocoDetecti on(root, annFile, transform)`	Loads images with COCO-style annotations.
2	Load Pre-trained Model	`models.detection.ssd lite320_mobilenet_v3 _large(pretrained=Tr ue)`	Loads a pre-trained SSD-Lite model.
3	Define Optimizer	`torch.optim.Adam(mod el.parameters(), lr=0.001)`	Configures the optimizer for training.
4	Perform Inference	`model.eval(); outputs = model(images)`	Runs the model on input data for predictions.
5	Display Detections	`cv2.rectangle(image, start, end, color, thickness)`	Draws bounding boxes on images.

Syntax Explanation:

1. Load Dataset

What is Loading a Dataset?
Loading a dataset retrieves labeled images and their annotations for training an object detector.

Syntax:

```
from torchvision import datasets, transforms

data_transforms = transforms.Compose([
    transforms.ToTensor()
])
dataset = datasets.CocoDetection(root="data/images",
annFile="data/annotations.json",
transform=data_transforms)
```

Detailed Explanation:

- **Purpose:** Provides labeled images and annotations for training.
- **Parameters:**
  - `root`: Directory containing the image files.
  - `annFile`: Path to the annotation file in COCO format.
  - `transform`: Preprocessing steps applied to the images.
- **Behavior:**
  - Associates each image with its bounding boxes and labels.
  - Prepares data for training or evaluation.
- **Output:** A dataset object compatible with PyTorch's `DataLoader`.

Example:
```
print(f"Number of images: {len(dataset)}")
```
Example Explanation:

- Displays the total number of images in the dataset.
- Confirms successful loading of the dataset.

2. Load Pre-trained Model

What is Loading a Pre-trained Model?

Loading a pre-trained model leverages state-of-the-art architectures trained on large datasets like COCO.

Syntax:
```
from torchvision import models

model =
models.detection.ssdlite320_mobilenet_v3_large(pretrain
ed=True)
```
Detailed Explanation:

- **Purpose:** Reduces training time by starting with a model pre-trained on a large dataset.
- **Parameters:**
  - `pretrained`: If True, loads weights trained on COCO.
- **Behavior:**
  - Initializes the model with pre-trained weights.
  - Outputs bounding boxes and class probabilities.
- **Output:** A ready-to-use object detection model.

Example:
```
print(model)
```
Example Explanation:
- Displays the architecture and components of the pre-trained model.
- Verifies the input and output configurations.

3. Define Optimizer

What is Defining an Optimizer?
The optimizer updates model parameters during training to minimize the loss function.
Syntax:
```
import torch.optim as optim

optimizer = optim.Adam(model.parameters(), lr=0.001)
```

Detailed Explanation:
- **Purpose:** Configures the optimization algorithm for training.
- **Parameters:**
  - parameters(): Model parameters to optimize.
  - lr: Learning rate for gradient updates.
- **Behavior:**
  - Adjusts weights based on gradients from the loss function.
- **Output:** An optimizer object ready for use in training.

Example:
```
print(optimizer)
```
Example Explanation:
- Displays the optimizer configuration, confirming learning rate and parameters.

4. Perform Inference

What is Performing Inference?
Inference uses a trained model to make predictions on input data.

Syntax:

```
model.eval()
with torch.no_grad():
    outputs = model(images)
```

Detailed Explanation:

- **Purpose:** Generates predictions for bounding boxes, class labels, and probabilities.
- **Steps:**
    - Switches the model to evaluation mode with `model.eval()`.
    - Processes input images to produce detection results.
- **Output:** A dictionary containing bounding boxes, labels, and scores for each image.

Example:

```
print(outputs)
```

Example Explanation:

- Displays the model's predictions, including bounding boxes and scores.

5. Display Detections

What is Displaying Detections?

Displaying detections involves visualizing the model's predictions by drawing bounding boxes on images.

Syntax:

```
import cv2
for box in outputs["boxes"]:
    start_point = (int(box[0]), int(box[1]))
    end_point = (int(box[2]), int(box[3]))
    cv2.rectangle(image, start_point, end_point,
color=(255, 0, 0), thickness=2)
```

Detailed Explanation:

- **Purpose:** Visualizes the detection results for easier interpretation.
- **Parameters:**
    - `start_point`: Top-left corner of the bounding box.
    - `end_point`: Bottom-right corner of the bounding box.
    - `color`: Color of the bounding box.

o   `thickness`: Thickness of the rectangle's border.
- **Output:** Annotated images with bounding boxes.

Example:

```
cv2.imshow("Detections", image)
cv2.waitKey(0)
```

Example Explanation:
- Displays the annotated image with detections.
- Confirms that the bounding boxes align with the model's predictions

Real-Life Project:

Project Name: Real-Time Object Detection System

Project Goal: Build and deploy a real-time object detection system for live video streams.

Code for This Project:

```
import torch
import cv2
from torchvision import models, transforms
# Load pre-trained model
model =
models.detection.ssdlite320_mobilenet_v3_large(pretrain
ed=True)
model.eval()
# Define transform
transform = transforms.Compose([
    transforms.ToTensor()
])
# Open video stream
cap = cv2.VideoCapture(0)
while cap.isOpened():
    ret, frame = cap.read()
    if not ret:
        break
    # Preprocess frame
    image = cv2.cvtColor(frame, cv2.COLOR_BGR2RGB)
    input_tensor = transform(image).unsqueeze(0)
```

```
    # Perform inference
    with torch.no_grad():
        outputs = model(input_tensor)
    # Draw detections
    for box, score, label in zip(outputs[0]['boxes'],
outputs[0]['scores'], outputs[0]['labels']):
        if score > 0.5:
            start_point = (int(box[0]), int(box[1]))
            end_point = (int(box[2]), int(box[3]))
            cv2.rectangle(frame, start_point,
end_point, (0, 255, 0), 2)

    # Display results
    cv2.imshow("Real-Time Object Detection", frame)
    if cv2.waitKey(1) & 0xFF == ord('q'):
        break

cap.release()
cv2.destroyAllWindows()
```

Expected Output:

- Displays a live video stream with real-time object detections.
- Annotates bounding boxes and labels on detected objects in the video feed.

Chapter - 41 Building a Chatbot with PyTorch

Chatbots are conversational agents designed to interact with users in natural language. PyTorch provides the tools to build both rule-based and machine learning-based chatbots, including those powered by sequence-to-sequence models or transformers. This chapter focuses on creating a chatbot using PyTorch, covering essential components like data preprocessing, model architecture, training, and deployment.

Key Characteristics of Chatbots:
- **Natural Language Understanding:** Interprets user input to determine intent and extract entities.
- **Response Generation:** Generates contextually relevant responses.
- **Customizability:** Supports rule-based, retrieval-based, and generative models.
- **Deployment:** Can integrate with messaging platforms and APIs.
- **Applications:** Customer support, virtual assistants, entertainment, and more.

Steps to Build a Chatbot:
1. **Collect and Preprocess Data:** Prepare conversational datasets by cleaning and tokenizing text.
2. **Design Model Architecture:** Choose between sequence-to-sequence (Seq2Seq), transformer-based, or rule-based models.
3. **Train the Model:** Optimize the model on conversational data.
4. **Evaluate the Model:** Measure performance using metrics like BLEU or perplexity.
5. **Deploy the Chatbot:** Integrate with a frontend for user interaction.

Syntax Table:

SL No	Function	Syntax/Example	Description
1	Tokenize Text	`tokenizer.encode(te xt, return_tensors='pt' )`	Converts text into token IDs for model input.
2	Define Seq2Seq Model	`nn.Transformer(d_mo del, nhead, num_layers)`	Creates a transformer-based chatbot model.
3	Train Model	`model.train()`	Optimizes the model on training data.
4	Generate Response	`model.generate(inpu t_ids, max_length)`	Generates a response to user input.
5	Save and Load Model	`torch.save(model.st ate_dict(), 'model.pth')`	Saves or loads the trained model.

Syntax Explanation:

1. Tokenize Text
What is Tokenizing Text?
Tokenization converts raw text into tokens or numerical IDs for processing by NLP models.
Syntax:
```
from transformers import AutoTokenizer

tokenizer = AutoTokenizer.from_pretrained("gpt2")
tokens = tokenizer.encode("Hello, how can I help you?",
return_tensors='pt')
```
Detailed Explanation:
- **Purpose:** Prepares raw text for processing by converting it into a format compatible with the model.
- **Parameters:**
  - text: The input string to tokenize.
  - return_tensors: Specifies the output format (e.g.,

PyTorch tensor).
- **Behavior:**
  - ○ Splits the input text into tokens.
  - ○ Maps tokens to their corresponding numerical IDs.
- **Output:** A tensor of token IDs ready for model input.

Example:
```
print(tokens)
```
Example Explanation:
- Displays the numerical representation of the input text.
- Confirms proper tokenization.

2. Define Seq2Seq Model

What is a Seq2Seq Model?
A sequence-to-sequence model processes input sequences (e.g., user queries) and generates output sequences (e.g., responses).
Syntax:
```
import torch.nn as nn

model = nn.Transformer(d_model=512, nhead=8,
num_encoder_layers=6, num_decoder_layers=6)
```
Detailed Explanation:
- **Purpose:** Encodes the input sequence and decodes it into an output sequence.
- **Parameters:**
  - ○ d_model: Dimensionality of the embeddings.
  - ○ nhead: Number of attention heads.
  - ○ num_encoder_layers: Number of layers in the encoder.
  - ○ num_decoder_layers: Number of layers in the decoder.
- **Behavior:**
  - ○ Captures context from the input sequence using self-attention.
  - ○ Generates responses conditioned on the input sequence.
- **Output:** A transformer-based chatbot model.

Example:
```
print(model)
```

Example Explanation:
- Displays the architecture of the Seq2Seq model.
- Verifies the model configuration.

3. Train Model

What is Training a Model?
Training a model involves optimizing its parameters using conversational data to minimize the loss function.
Syntax:

```
model.train()
for input_ids, target_ids in data_loader:
    optimizer.zero_grad()
    outputs = model(input_ids, labels=target_ids)
    loss = outputs.loss
    loss.backward()
    optimizer.step()
```

Detailed Explanation:
- **Purpose:** Learns to generate accurate and relevant responses by minimizing loss.
- **Steps:**
  - Sets the model to training mode with `model.train()`.
  - Processes input-output pairs through the model.
  - Computes loss and updates weights using backpropagation.
- **Output:** A trained chatbot model.

Example:

```
print(f"Loss: {loss.item():.4f}")
```

Example Explanation:
- Logs the training loss for monitoring progress.

4. Generate Response

What is Generating a Response?
Generating a response uses the trained model to produce conversational output based on user input.

Syntax:

```
response = model.generate(input_ids, max_length=50)
```

Detailed Explanation:

- **Purpose:** Produces a coherent response to the user's query.
- **Parameters:**
  - `input_ids`: Tokenized user input.
  - `max_length`: Maximum length of the generated response.
- **Behavior:**
  - Generates tokens one by one, conditioned on the input.
- **Output:** A sequence of token IDs representing the response.

Example:

```
decoded_response = tokenizer.decode(response[0],
skip_special_tokens=True)
print(decoded_response)
```

Example Explanation:

- Converts token IDs back to text for readability.
- Confirms the model's ability to generate coherent responses.

5. Save and Load Model

What is Saving and Loading a Model?

Saving a trained model preserves its parameters, allowing it to be reloaded for future use.

Syntax:

```
torch.save(model.state_dict(), 'chatbot_model.pth')
model.load_state_dict(torch.load('chatbot_model.pth'))
```

Detailed Explanation:

- **Purpose:** Ensures model reusability without retraining.
- **Steps:**
  - Saves the model's state dictionary to a file.
  - Loads the state dictionary into the model.
- **Output:** A saved and reloaded model ready for inference.

Example:

```
print("Model saved and loaded successfully.")
```

Example Explanation:

- Confirms that the model's state has been saved and restored.

Real-Life Project:

Project Name: AI Customer Support Chatbot

Project Goal: Build a chatbot to assist customers by answering frequently asked questions and providing support.

Code for This Project:

```python
from transformers import AutoModelForCausalLM,
AutoTokenizer
import torch

# Load pre-trained model and tokenizer
model =
AutoModelForCausalLM.from_pretrained("microsoft/DialoGP
T-medium")
tokenizer =
AutoTokenizer.from_pretrained("microsoft/DialoGPT-
medium")
# Chat loop
print("Start chatting with the bot! Type 'exit' to
end.")
while True:
    user_input = input("You: ")
    if user_input.lower() == 'exit':
        break
    input_ids = tokenizer.encode(user_input +
tokenizer.eos_token, return_tensors='pt')
    response_ids = model.generate(input_ids,
max_length=50, pad_token_id=tokenizer.eos_token_id)
    response = tokenizer.decode(response_ids[:,
input_ids.shape[-1]:][0], skip_special_tokens=True)
    print(f"Bot: {response}")
```

Expected Output:

- Engages in a back-and-forth conversation with the user.
- Generates contextually relevant responses to user input.

www.ingramcontent.com/pod-product-compliance
Lightning Source LLC
Chambersburg PA
CBHW070938050326
40689CB00014B/3253